Beginning Java Data Structures and Algorithms

Sharpen your problem solving skills by learning core computer science concepts in a pain-free manner

James Cutajar

BIRMINGHAM - MUMBAI

Beginning Java Data Structures and Algorithms

Acquisitions Editor: Aditya Date, Bridget Neale
Content Development Editors: Madhura Bal, Madhunikita Sunil Chindarkar
Production Coordinator: Ratan Pote

First published: July 2018

Production reference: 1270718

Published by Packt Publishing Ltd.
Livery Place
35 Livery Street
Birmingham
B3 2PB, UK.

ISBN 978-1-78953-717-8

www.packtpub.com

`mapt.io`

Mapt is an online digital library that gives you full access to over 5,000 books and videos, as well as industry leading tools to help you plan your personal development and advance your career. For more information, please visit our website.

Why Subscribe?

- Spend less time reading and more time coding with practical eBooks and Videos from over 4,000 industry professionals
- Improve your learning with Skill Plans built especially for you
- Get a free eBook or video every month
- Mapt is fully searchable
- Copy and paste, print, and bookmark content

PacktPub.com

Did you know that Packt offers eBook versions of every book published, with PDF and ePub files available? You can upgrade to the eBook version at `www.PacktPub.com` and as a print book customer, you are entitled to a discount on the eBook copy. Get in touch with us at `service@packtpub.com` for more details.

At `www.PacktPub.com`, you can also read a collection of free technical articles, sign up for a range of free newsletters, and receive exclusive discounts and offers on Packt books and eBooks.

Contributors

About the Author

James Cutajar is a software developer with an interest in scalable, high-performance computing, and distributed algorithms. He is also an author, open source contributor, blogger, and a tech evangelist. When he is not writing software, he is riding his motorbike, surfing, or flying light aircraft. He was born in Malta, lived in London for almost a decade, and is now working in Portugal.

Packt Is Searching for Authors like You

If you're interested in becoming an author for Packt, please visit authors.packtpub.com and apply today. We have worked with thousands of developers and tech professionals, just like you, to help them share their insight with the global tech community. You can make a general application, apply for a specific hot topic that we are recruiting an author for, or submit your own idea.

Table of Contents

Preface

A data structure is a way of organizing data so that it can be accessed and/or modified efficiently. Learning about data structures and algorithms gives you a better insight on how to solve common programming problems. Most of the problems faced everyday by programmers have been solved, tried and tested. Knowing how these solutions work, ensures that the right tool is chosen when faced with these problems.

This book teaches you tools that you can use to build efficient applications. It starts with an introduction to algorithms and big O notation, later explains bubble, merge, quicksort, and other popular programming patterns. You'll also learn about data structures such as binary trees, hash tables, and graphs. The book progresses to advanced concepts, such as algorithm design paradigms and graph theory. By the end of the book, you will know how to correctly implement common algorithms and data structures within your applications.

Who This Book Is For

If you want to better understand common data structures and algorithms by following code examples in Java and improve your application efficiency, then this is the book for you. It helps to have basic knowledge of Java, mathematics and object-oriented programming techniques.

What This Book Covers

Chapter 1, *Algorithms and Complexities*, covers how to define an algorithm, measure algorithmic complexity, and identify algorithms with different complexities. It also covers how to assess various examples with different runtime complexities

Chapter 2, *Sorting Algorithms and Fundamental Data Structures*, explores bubble, quick, and merge sort. We will also introduce data structures and study various implementations and use cases of linked lists, queues, and stacks. We will also see how some data structures can be used as building blocks to build more complex ones.

Chapter 3, *Hash Tables and Binary Search Trees*, talks about data structures for implementing the data dictionary operation. In addition, binary trees also give us the ability to perform various range queries. We will also see examples of both data structures, and implementations of these operations.

Chapter 4, *Algorithm Design Paradigms*, discusses three different algorithm design paradigms along with example problems, and discusses how to identify whether problems may be solvable by one of the given paradigms.

Chapter 5, *String Matching Algorithms*, introduces the string matching problem. This chapter also introduces you to the string matching algorithms, starting from the naive search algorithm and improving it by using the rules introduced by Boyer and Moore. We'll also explore some other string matching algorithms without going into too much detail about them.

Chapter 6, *Graphs, Prime Numbers, and Complexity Classes*, introduces graphs, formalizing what they are and showing two different ways to represent them in computer programs. Later, we'll take a look at ways of traversing graphs, using them as building blocks for building more complex algorithms. We'll also look at two different algorithms for finding shortest paths in a graph.

To Get the Most out of This Book

For successful completion of this book, you will require a computer system with at least an i3 processor, 4 GB RAM, 10 GB hard disk and an internet connection. Along with this you would require the following software:

- Java SE Development Kit, JDK 8 (or a later version)
- Git client
- Java IDE (IntelliJ or Eclipse)

Download the Example Code Files

You can download the example code files for this book from your account at
www.packtpub.com. If you purchased this book elsewhere, you can visit
www.packtpub.com/support and register to have the files emailed directly to you.

You can download the code files by following these steps:

1. Log in or register at www.packtpub.com.
2. Select the **SUPPORT** tab.
3. Click on **Code Downloads & Errata**.
4. Enter the name of the book in the **Search** box and follow the onscreen instructions.

Once the file is downloaded, please make sure that you unzip or extract the folder using the latest version of:

- WinRAR/7-Zip for Windows
- Zipeg/iZip/UnRarX for Mac
- 7-Zip/PeaZip for Linux

The code bundle for the book is also hosted on GitHub at https://github.com/
TrainingByPackt/Data-Structures-and-Algorithms-in-Java. In case there's an update to
the code, it will be updated on the existing GitHub repository.

We also have other code bundles from our rich catalog of books and videos available
at https://github.com/PacktPublishing/. Check them out!

Download the Color Images

We also provide a PDF file that has color images of the screenshots/diagrams used in this
book. You can download it here: https://www.packtpub.com/sites/default/files/
downloads/BeginningJavaDataStructuresandAlgorithms_ColorImages.pdf.

Conventions Used

There are a number of text conventions used throughout this book.

CodeInText: Indicates code words in text, database table names, folder names, filenames, file extensions, pathnames, dummy URLs, user input, and Twitter handles. Here is an example: "This is the task of the merge() function, which is found at the end of the pseudocode shown in the preceding section."

A block of code is set as follows:

```
quickSort(array, start, end)
if(start < end)
p = partition(array, start, end)
quickSort(array, start, p - 1)
quickSort(array, p + 1, end)
```

Any command-line input or output is written as follows:

```
gradlew test --tests
com.packt.datastructuresandalg.lesson2.activity.selectionsort*
```

Bold: Indicates a new term, an important word, or words that you see on screen. For example, words in menus or dialog boxes appear in the text like this. Here is an example: "Select **Dynamic Web Project** and click **Next** to open the **Dynamic Web Project** wizard."

Activity: These are scenario-based activities that will let you practically apply what you've learned over the course of a complete section. They are typically in the context of a real-world problem or situation.

 Warnings or important notes appear like this.

Get in Touch

Feedback from our readers is always welcome.

General feedback: Email `feedback@packtpub.com` and mention the book title in the subject of your message. If you have questions about any aspect of this book, please email us at `questions@packtpub.com`.

Errata: Although we have taken every care to ensure the accuracy of our content, mistakes do happen. If you have found a mistake in this book, we would be grateful if you would report this to us. Please visit `www.packtpub.com/submit-errata`, selecting your book, clicking on the Errata Submission Form link, and entering the details.

Piracy: If you come across any illegal copies of our works in any form on the Internet, we would be grateful if you would provide us with the location address or website name. Please contact us at `copyright@packtpub.com` with a link to the material.

If you are interested in becoming an author: If there is a topic that you have expertise in and you are interested in either writing or contributing to a book, please visit `authors.packtpub.com`.

Reviews

Please leave a review. Once you have read and used this book, why not leave a review on the site that you purchased it from? Potential readers can then see and use your unbiased opinion to make purchase decisions, we at Packt can understand what you think about our products, and our authors can see your feedback on their book. Thank you!

For more information about Packt, please visit `packtpub.com`.

Algorithms and Complexities 1

An algorithm is a set of logical instructions to perform a particular task. Algorithms are everywhere nowadays. As a software developer, understanding the core principles of algorithms and data structures will enable you to make informed decisions on how to approach a particular problem. This is valid whether you're working in a bank writing accounting software or doing medical research data, mining genetic code. How do we determine which is the right algorithm to use when more than one solution to a problem exists? In this chapter, we will examine different types of algorithms and discuss how the performance varies in each. We will discuss what makes an algorithm more efficient than another and how to express the complexity of each.

The common examples of algorithms include traffic lights regulating congestion on the streets, face recognition software on smartphones, recommendation technologies, and so on.
It's important for you to understand that an algorithm is just a small part of an application used to solve a well-defined problem. Examples such as sorting a list of numbers, finding the shortest route, or word prediction are all correct. Big software applications, such as email clients or an operating system are improper examples.

By the end of this chapter, you will be able to:

- Define an algorithm with an example
- Measure algorithmic complexity
- Identify algorithms with different complexities
- Assess various examples with different runtime complexities

Developing Our First Algorithm

An algorithm can be seen as a roadmap or a set of instructions to accomplish a well-defined task. In this section, we will build a simple example of one such algorithm to help us get started.

Algorithm for Converting Binary Numbers to Decimal

Number systems have different bases. Decimals numbers with a base of ten are what most of us are familiar with. Computers, on the other hand, use only ones and zeros (binary). Let's try to write some code that converts binary numbers to decimals.

Specifically, we want to develop an algorithm that accepts a string containing ones and zeros and returns an integer.

We can convert the binary string by following these steps:

1. Start from the end of the string and process each character at a time. The position of each digit in the binary string corresponds to a decimal number in a sequence.
2. To generate this sequence, you start from one and multiply by two every time, so one, two, four, eight, and so on (see *Conversion Sequence* row of *Table 1.1*). More formally, the sequence is a geometric progression that starts at one and progresses in a common ratio of two.
3. We then apply the binary string as a mask on this sequence (see the *Binary String (Mask)* row of *Table 1.1*).
4. The result is a new sequence where the values are only kept if the corresponding position in the binary string has a value of one (see the *Result* row of *Table 1.1*).
5. After applying the mask, we just need to sum up the resulting numbers together.

Conversion Sequence	16	8	4	2	1
Binary String (Mask)	1	0	1	1	0
Result	16	0	4	2	0

Table 1.1: Binary to decimal masking

In the preceding example (*Table 1.1*), resulting total is **22**. This is our decimal number corresponding to the binary number 10110.

To design our algorithm, it's important to realize that we don't need to store the entire conversion sequence. Since we are processing one binary digit at a time (starting from the back), we only need to use the conversion number corresponding to the binary position we are processing.

Snippet 1.1 shows us how we can do this. We use a single conversion variable instead of a sequence and initialize this variable to the value of one. We then use a loop to iterate over the length of the binary string starting from the end. While iterating, if the digit at our current position is one, we add the current conversion variable to the final result. We then simply double the current conversion variable and repeat. The code snippet is as follows:

```
public int convertToDecimal(String binary) {
    int conversion = 1;
    int result = 0;
    for (int i = 1; i <= binary.length(); i++) {
        if (binary.charAt(binary.length() - i) == '1')
            result += conversion;
        conversion *= 2;
    }
    return result;
}
```

Snippet 1.1: Binary to decimal. Source class name: BinaryToDecimal.

Go to `https://goo.gl/rETLfq` to access the code.

Activity: Writing an Algorithm to Convert Numbers from Octal To Decimal

Scenario

In aviation, the aircraft's transponders transmit a code so that they can identify one another. This code uses the octal system, a number system which has a base of 8. We have been asked to write a method to convert octal numbers into decimals. For example, the octal number 17 is represented as 15 in the decimal system.

Aim

To be able to adapt the algorithm shown in the previous section to be used in a different scenario.

Prerequisites

- Ensure that you have a class available on the following path:

    ```
    https://github.com/TrainingByPackt/Data-Structures-and-Algorithms-in-J
    ava/blob/master/src/main/java/com/packt/datastructuresandalg/lesson1/a
    ctivity/octaltodecimal/OctalToDecimal.java
    ```

- You will find the following method that needs implementing:

    ```
    public int convertToDecimal (String octal)
    ```

- If you have your project set up, you can run the unit test for this activity by running the following command:

    ```
    gradlew test --tests com.packt.datastructuresandalg.
    lesson1.activity.octaltodecimal*
    ```

Steps for Completion

1. The algorithms shown in *Snippet 1.1* the preceding snippets of code can be adapted to work with octal numbers instead of binary.
2. Change the base from two to eight. This can be done by changing the conversion multiplier variable in *Snippet 1.1*.
3. Parse the digit being processed to convert it into an integer. This integer can then be multiplied by the conversion variable or result of the power function.

In this first section, we introduced the idea of algorithms by working on a simple example. It's important to note that for every problem multiple solutions exist. Choosing the right algorithm to solve your problem will depend on several metrics, such as performance and memory requirements.

Measuring Algorithmic Complexity with Big O Notation

Algorithmic complexity is a way to describe the efficiency of an algorithm as a relation of its input. It can be used to describe various properties of our code, such as runtime speed or memory requirements. It's also a very important tool programmers should understand to write efficient software. In this section, we will start by describing a scenario, introducing the section, and then dive into the details of the various types of complexities and the different techniques to measure them.

Complexity Example

Imagine we were given the task of writing a piece of software for air traffic control. Specifically, we were asked to write an algorithm that, in a pre-defined space and altitude, will ring out an alarm if any two aircraft get too close to each other.

In our implementation, we solved the problem by computing all possible distances between every pair in our airspace and keeping only the minimum distance. If this minimum distance is less than a certain threshold, our software will ring out an alarm. The following snippet of code shows this solution:

```
public double minimumDistance(List<Point> allPlanes) {
    double minDistance = Double.MAX_VALUE;
    for (Point p1 : allPlanes) {
        for (Point p2 : allPlanes) {
            double d = p1.distanceTo(p2);
            if (d != 0 && d < minDistance) minDistance = d;
        }
    }
    return minDistance;
}
```

Snippet 1.2: Minimum distance. Source class name: ClosestPlane and Point.

Note that the `Point` class in the preceding piece of code is not shown. Go to `https://goo.gl/iDHD5J` to access the code.

Our little algorithm works fine for a couple of years and the controllers are happy to have this useful alerting. However, over the years, air traffic increases at a fast rate, and instead of having to monitor a few hundred aircraft at any given time, our algorithm has to handle tens of thousands of points. At busy times, the software is having trouble keeping up with the increased load.

We are called in to investigate and we start to write some benchmarks to test how fast the algorithm performs. We obtain the timings shown in *Table 1.2*. As you can see, we are doubling the load on every run; however, our algorithm is not scaling up in the same manner. Our algorithm is not slowing down at the same rate as our input.

Intuitively, you may expect that if you double the number of planes, the algorithm has, then you have twice the amount of work to do, and as a result, it should take twice as long. However, this is not what is happening.

When we double the number of planes, the time taken doesn't just double but skyrockets.

For example, our algorithm takes 2.6 seconds (2,647 ms) to finish when it's dealing with 16,000 planes. However, if we double the amount of planes to 32,000, the time it takes increases to 10.4 seconds (10,488 ms), a four-fold increase!

Number of planes	Time taken (ms)
1000	27
2000	48
4000	190
8000	664
16000	2647
32000	10488

In the following graph, we plot the benchmark results in a chart. What is going on here? Our algorithm is doing a lot of work due to the nested loop. For every plane point in its input, it's calculating the distance to every other plane. This results in n^2 calculations, where n is the number of planes we are monitoring. We can say that our algorithm has a runtime performance of $O(n^2)$, read as *big O of n squared*. Alternatively, we can also call it the quadratic runtime performance. Take a look at this graph:

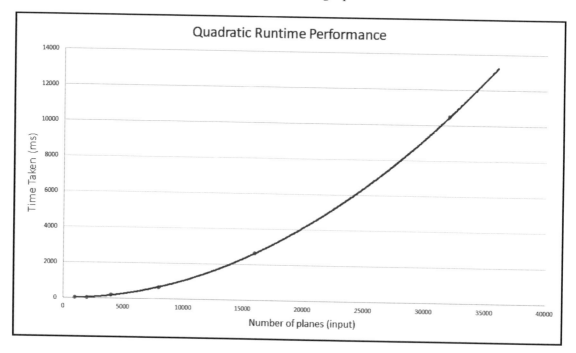

Figure 1.1: Algorithm benchmark result plot

The algorithm listed in *Snippet 1.2* is a slow solution for the closest pair problem. There exists a much more efficient solution that involves a divide and conquer technique.

This class of algorithms is explored in detail in the second part of this book in `Chapter 4`, *Algorithm Design Paradigms*, where we present a faster solution to the closest pair problem.

Increasing the input load on your code does not always mean that the resource consumption will also increase in a directly proportional manner. The relation between the input size of your problem and resource usage (CPU time, memory, and so on) is what this section is all about.

In the next section, we will see different types of these relations between the problem, input size, and resource usage.

Understanding Complexity

To better understand algorithmic complexity, we can make use of an analogy. Imagine that we were to set different types of algorithms so that they compete against one another on a race track. However, there is a slight twist: The race course has no finish line.

Since the race is infinite, the aim of the race is to surpass the other, slower opponents over time and not to finish first. In this analogy, the race track distance is our algorithm input. How far from the start we get, after a certain amount of time, represents the amount of work done by our code.

Recall the quadratic method for measuring the closest pair of planes in the preceding section. In our fictitious race, the quadratic algorithm starts quite fast and is able to move quite a distance before it starts slowing down, similar to a runner that is getting tired and slowing down. The further it gets away from the start line, the slower it gets, although it never stops moving.

Not only do the algorithms progress through the race at different speeds, but their way of moving varies from one type to another. We already mentioned that $O(n^2)$ solutions slow down as they progress along the race. How does this compare to the others?

Another type of runner taking part in our imaginary race is the linear algorithm. Linear algorithms are described with the notation of $O(n)$. Their speed on our race track is constant. Think of them as an old, reliable car moving at the same fixed speed.

In real life, solutions that have an $O(n)$ runtime complexity have a running performance that is directly proportional to the size of their input.

This means, for example, that if you double the input size of a linear algorithm, the algorithm would also take about twice as long to finish.

The efficiency of each algorithm is always evaluated in the long run. Given a big enough input, a linear algorithm will always perform better than a quadratic one.

We can go much quicker than $O(n)$. Imagine that our algorithm is continually accelerating along the track instead of moving constantly. This is the opposite of quadratic runtime. Given enough distance, these solutions can get really fast. We say that these type of algorithms have a logarithmic complexity written as $O(log\ n)$.

In real life, this means that the algorithm doesn't slow much as the size of the input increases. Again, it doesn't matter if at the start, the algorithm performs slower than a linear one for a small input, as for a big enough input, a logarithmic solution will always outperform the linear one.

Can we go even faster? It turns out that there is another complexity class of algorithms that performs even better.

Picture a runner in our race who has the ability to teleport in constant time to any location along our infinite track. Even if the teleportation takes a long time, as long as it's constant and doesn't depend on the distance traveled, this type of runner will always beat any other. No matter how long the teleportation takes, given enough distance, the algorithm will always arrive there first. This is what is known as a constant runtime complexity, written as $O(1)$. Solutions that belong to this complexity class will have a runtime independent of the input size given.

On the other side of the spectrum, we can find algorithms that are much slower than quadratic ones. Complexities such as cubic with $O(n^3)$ or quartic with $O(n^4)$ are examples. All of the mentioned complexities up to this point are said to be polynomial complexities.

A polynomial is simply a mathematical term used for expressions. Expressions such as $3x^5 + 2x^3 + 6$, $2x - 3$, or even just 5 are all good examples. The key here is that polynomial complexities are of the form $O(n^k)$, where k is a positive, non-fractional constant.

Not all solutions have a polynomial time behavior. A particular class of algorithms scale really badly in proportion to their input with a runtime performance of $O(k^n)$. In this class, the efficiency degrades exponentially with the input size. All the other types of polynomial algorithms will outperform any exponential one pretty fast. *Figure 1.2* shows how this type of behavior compares with the previously mentioned polynomial algorithms.

The following graph also shows how fast an exponential algorithm degrades with input size:

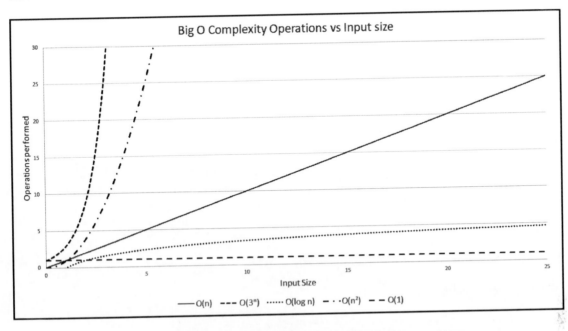

Figure 1.2: Operations performed versus input size for different algorithms

How much faster does a logarithmic algorithm perform versus a quadratic one? Let's try to pick a particular example. A specific algorithm performs about two operations to solve a problem; however, the relation to its input is $O(n^2)$.

Assuming each operation is a slow one (such as file access) and has a constant time of about 0.25 milliseconds, the time required to perform those operations will be as shown in *Table 1.3*. We work out the timings by $Time = 0.25 * operations * n^2$, where operations is the number of operations performed (in this example it's equal to 2), n is the input size, and *0.25* is the time taken per operation:

Input Size (n)	Time: 2 operations $O(n^2)$	Time: 400 operations $O(\log n)$
10	50 milliseconds	100 milliseconds
100	5 seconds	200 milliseconds
1000	8.3 minutes	300 milliseconds
10000	13.8 hours	400 milliseconds

Table 1.3: How fast does it run?

Our logarithmic algorithm performs around 400 operations; however, its relation to the input size is logarithmic. Although this algorithm is slower for a smaller input, it quickly overtakes the quadratic algorithm. You can notice that, with a large enough input, the difference in performance is huge. In this case, we work out the timing using *Time = 0.25 * operations * log n*, with *operations = 400*.

Activity: Developing a Timing Table Using the Exponential Algorithm

Scenario

We have been asked to develop a timing table using an input size of 2, 10, 30, and 50 for an exponential algorithm of $O(2^n)$. Assume an operation time of 0.5 ms and that the algorithm only performs one operation.

Aim

To discover how badly exponential algorithms scale.

Steps for Completion

1. $0.5 \times 2^2 = 2$ ms
2. $0.5 \times 2^{10} = 512$ ms
3. $0.5 \times 2^{30} = 0.536$ billion ms = 6.2 days
4. $0.5 \times 2^{50} = 5.629$ and 10^{14} ms = 17838 years

Output

The results may be as follows:

Input Size (n)	Time : 1 Operations $O(2^n)$
2	2 milliseconds
10	512 milliseconds
30	6.2 days
50	17838 years

Table 1.4: Timings for the $O(2^n)$ algorithm

In this section, we have compared different types of algorithmic runtime complexities. We have seen how each compares against the others, starting from the theory's fastest of *O(1)* to some of the slowest with *O(kⁿ)*. It's also important to understand that there is a difference between theory and practice. For example, in real life, a quadratic algorithm may outperform a linear one if the operations performed are less, the input is a fixed size, and is small.

Complexity Notation

In the previous section, we have seen how we can use the big O notation to measure the runtime performance to our algorithms in proportion to the input size. We have neither examined in detail what *O(n)* really means nor have we considered the performance of our algorithm in relation to the type of input it's given.

Consider the following code snippet. The method accepts an array containing a string and searches for a match. If one is found, the index of the array is returned. We will use this example and try to measure the runtime complexity. The code is as follows:

```
public int search(String strToMatch, String[] strArray) {
    for (int i = 0; i < strArray.length; i++) {
        if (strArray[i].equals(strToMatch)) {
            return i;
        }
    }
    return -1;
}
```

Snippet 1.3: Array search. Source class name: ArraySearch.

Go to `https://goo.gl/egw1Sn` to access the code.

There are a number of operations happening inside the loop. The obvious ones are the arrays accessing at `i` and the string `equals`. However, we also have the increment of `i`, the assignment of the new incremented value to `i` and the comparison of `i` being less than the length of the array. However, this is not the end of the story. The `equals()` method is also matching each character of the string to an element at `i` in the array.

The following table lists all these operations:

Operation name	Code	Count
Array access	`strArray[i]`	1
String equality	`.equals(strToMatch)`	String length
Array pointer increment and assignment	`i = i + 1`	2
Reading array length and comparing to pointer	`i < strArray.length`	2

Table 1.5: Operations performed in the ArraySearch method for every item

We have seen that for each processed item in the search array, we perform $5 + m$ operations, where m is the length of the search string. The next aspect to look at is to work out how often we perform this. The number of times we perform the operations mentioned in *Table 1.5* doesn't just rely on the length of our input; it also depends on how quick we are in finding our match in the input array, that is, it depends on the actual array's contents.

 The best case of an algorithm is when the input causes the algorithm to perform in the most efficient manner possible. The worst case is the opposite, which is when a particular input makes it behave in the least efficient manner possible.

If we are lucky and the item we are searching for is located in the first element of the search array, we perform only $5 + m$ operations. This is the best case and is the fastest manner our search can compute.

The worst case of this algorithm is either when our item is at the end of the array or when the item is not found at all. Both of these scenarios will have us then check the entire contents of the array. In the worst case, we end up performing $n(5 + m)$ operations, where n is the array size.

In this example, we can say that the worst-case runtime complexity for our algorithm is $O(mn)$ and our best case, when our algorithm finds a match immediately, is $O(m)$. We will see in the following sub-section how we arrive at this result from $5 + m$ and $n(5 + m)$.

Another algorithmic analysis that is commonly used is the average case performance. The average case complexity can be found by averaging the performance over all possible inputs. This is useful, as in certain scenarios, the worst case has a low chance of occurring.

Although we have the best, average, and worst-case complexities, the worst case is usually the most used when measuring and comparing different algorithms to one another. Apart from runtime performance, the other most common use of big O notation is to measure memory requirements. However, it can be used for any resource, such as disk space or network usage.

Identifying the Best and Worst Performance of an Algorithm While Checking for Duplicates in an Array

We want to determine the complexity of an algorithm checking for duplicates in an array by considering the best and worst case performance. Find the number of operations performed in the *Snippet 1.4* for both the worst and best case. There is no need to work out the algorithmic complexity in big O notation. Assume that the inner loop results in eight operations every time it executes.

For the outer loop, assume four operations:

```
public boolean containsDuplicates(int[] numbers) {
    for (int i=0; i<numbers.length; i++) {
        for (int j=0; j<numbers.length; j++) {
            if (i != j && numbers[i] == numbers[j]) return true;
        }
    }
    return false;
}
```

Snippet 1.4: Checking for duplicates. Source class name: Duplicates.

Go to `https://goo.gl/wEUqYk` to access the code.

To do this, we should perform the following steps:

1. In the worst- case, we execute the inner loop *n* times (array length).
2. In the best case, we only execute the inner loop only twice.
3. The best case is when the duplicate numbers are in the front of the input array. The worst is when the array doesn't contain any duplicates.

4. The worst case is when the array doesn't contain duplicates and is of size n:
   - For the outer loop, we have $4*n$ operations
   - For the inner loop, we have $n*(n*8)$ operations
   - In total, we have $4n + 8n^2$ operations

5. In the best case, the duplicates are the first two items in the array:
   - For the outer loop, we have 4 operations
   - For the inner loop, we have $2*8$ operations as the inner loop executes twice to get to the second item in the array where the duplicate is located
   - In total, we have 20 operations

We have seen how we can analyze the number of operations performed in an algorithm and how we can use big O notation to describe the best and worst case. We also discussed how the notation can be used to describe any resource usage. In the next section, we'll describe some basic rules that are used when using the notation.

Notation Rules

There are two simple rules to follow when we want to express an algorithm using the big O notation. In this section, we will understand how to convert the expression from $4n + 8n^2$ to the big O notation equivalent.

The first rule to follow is to drop any constants.

For example, $3n + 4$ becomes n and, a single constant such as 5 becomes 1. If an algorithm simply has 4 constant instructions that don't depend on the input, we say the algorithm is $O(1)$, also known as **constant time complexity**.

The second rule is to drop everything except the highest order.

 To understand why we adopt the second rule, it's important to realize that for a large value of n, anything but the highest order becomes irrelevant. When we have a large enough input, the performance difference is negligible.

Consider an algorithm that performs $n + n^2 + n^3$. The highest order variable of this is the n^3 part. If we keep the highest order, we end up with a big O runtime complexity of $O(n^3)$.

Activity: Converting Expressions to Big O Notations

Scenario

To convert the expression $3mn + 5mn^4 + 2n^2 + 6$ to a big O notation, firstly we drop any constants from the expression, leaving us with $mn+mn^4+n^2$. Next, we simply keep the highest order part, which results in $O(mn^4)$.

For each of the expressions found in *Table 1.6*, find the equivalent in big O notation:

Expression	$3mn$	$5n + 44n^2 + 4$	$4 + 5 \log n$	$3^n + 5n^2 + 8$

Table 1.6: Find big O equivalent

Aim

To apply notation rules to convert expressions into big O notations.

Steps for completion

1. Identify and drop the constants in the expression:
   - $3mn \rightarrow$ *No constants* $\rightarrow 3mn$
   - $5n + 44n^2 + 4 \rightarrow 4 \rightarrow 5n + 44n^2$
   - $4 + 5 \log n \rightarrow 4 \rightarrow 5 \log n$
   - $3^n + 5n^2 + 8 \rightarrow 8 \rightarrow 3^n + 5n^2$

2. Drop everything except the highest-order part:
   - $3mn \rightarrow O(mn)$
   - $5n + 44n^2 \rightarrow O(n^2)$
   - $5 \log n \rightarrow O(\log n)$
   - $3^n + 5n^2 \rightarrow O(3^n)$

Output

The outcome may be as follows:

Expression	$3mn$	$5n + 44n^2 + 4$	$4 + 5 \log n$	$3^n + 5n^2 + 8$
Solution	$O(mn)$	$O(n^2)$	$O(\log n)$	$O(3^n)$

Table 1.7: Solution to find big O equivalent activity

In this section, we have explored two simple rules used for converting expressions to big O notations. We have also learned why we keep only the highest-order from the expression. In the next section, we shall see some examples of algorithms with different complexities.

Identifying Algorithms with Different Complexities

In this section, we shall look into examples of different complexities. This is important so that we can learn to recognize algorithms that belong to different complexity classes and possibly attempt improving the performance of each.

 Figuring out the worst case complexity can be quite difficult for some algorithms. Sometimes, this requires some experience and is best learned by looking at many examples and getting familiar with different types of algorithms.

Linear Complexity

Linear algorithms are the ones where the work done varies in direct proportion with the input size, that is, if you double the input size, you double the work done. These typically involve a single pass through the input.

The problem presented in this example is that of counting the number of occurrences of a particular character in a string. Imagine we are given the string *Sally sells sea shells on the seashore*, and we want to find out the number of occurrences of the letter *a*.

The following code in *Snippet 1.5* goes through each character in the input string and if the character at the current position matches the search letter, a counter is increased. At the end of the loop, the final count is returned. The code is as follows:

```java
public int countChars(char c, String str) {
    int count = 0;
    for (int i = 0; i < str.length(); i++) {
        if (str.charAt(i) == c) count++;
    }
    return count;
}
```

Snippet 1.5: Count the number of characters in a string. Source class name: CountChars.

Go to `https://goo.gl/M4Vy7Y` to access the code.

Linear complexity algorithms are the most common types of algorithms. These usually make a single pass on the input and thus scale proportionally with the input size. In this section, we have seen one such example.

 The algorithm is linear because its runtime is directly proportional to the string length. If we take the string length to be n, the runtime complexity of this Java method is $O(n)$. Notice the single loop varying according to the input size. This is very typical of linear runtime complexity algorithms, where a constant number of operations are performed for each input unit. The input unit in this example is each character in the string.

Quadratic Complexity

Quadratic complexity algorithms are not very performant for large input sizes. The work done increases following a quadratic proportion as we increase our input size. We already saw an example of a $O(n^2)$ in our minimum distance solution in *Snippet 1.2*. There are many other examples, such as bubble and selection sorting. The problem presented in this example is about finding the common elements contained in two arrays (assuming no duplicate values exist in each array), producing the intersection of the two inputs. This results in a runtime complexity of $O(mn)$, where m and n are the sizes of the first and second input arrays. If the input arrays are the same size as n elements, this results in a runtime of $O(n^2)$. This can be demonstrated with the help of the following code:

```java
public List<Integer> intersection(int[] a, int[] b) {
  List<Integer> result = new ArrayList<>(a.length);
  for (int x : a) {
    for (int y : b) {
      if (x == y) result.add(x);
    }
  }
  return result;
}
```

Snippet 1.6: Intersection between two arrays. Source class name: SimpleIntersection.

Go to `https://goo.gl/uHuP5B` to access the code. There is a more efficient implementation of the intersection problem. This involves sorting the array first, resulting in an overall runtime of *O(n log n)*.

When calculating the space complexity, the memory consumed for the input arguments should be ignored. Only memory allocated inside the algorithms should be considered.

The amount of memory we use is dictated by the size of our result listed in our method. The bigger this list, the more memory we're using.

The best case is when we use the least amount of memory. This is when the list is empty, that is, when we have no common elements between the two arrays. Thus, this method has a best case space complexity of *O(1)*, when there is no intersection.

The worst case is just the opposite, when we have all the elements in both arrays. This can happen when the arrays are equal to each other, although the numbers may be in a different order. The memory in this case is equal to the size of one of our input arrays. In short, the worst space complexity of the method is *O(n)*.

In this section, we have shown examples of quadratic algorithms. Many other examples exist. In the next chapter, we will also describe a poorly-performing sorting algorithm, which is $O(n^2)$, called **bubble sort**.

Logarithmic Complexity

Logarithmic complexity algorithms are very fast, and their performance hardly degrades as you increase the problem size. These types of algorithm scale really well. Code that has a runtime complexity of *O(log n)* is usually recognizable since it systematically divides the input in several steps. Common examples that operate in logarithmic times are database indexes and binary trees. If we want to find an item in a list, we can do it much more efficiently if the input list is sorted in some specific order. We can then use this ordering by jumping to specific positions of our list and skipping over a number of elements.

Snippet 1.7 shows an implementation of the binary search in Java. The method uses three array pointers—a start, an end, and a midpoint. The algorithm starts by checking the middle element in the array. If the element is not found and is less than the value at the middle, we choose to search in the lower half; otherwise, we choose the upper half. *Figure 1.3* shows the steps involved when doing a binary search. The code snippet is as follows:

```java
public boolean binarySearch(int x, int[] sortedNumbers) {
    int end = sortedNumbers.length - 1;
    int start = 0;
    while (start <= end) {
        int mid = (end - start) / 2 + start;
        if (sortedNumbers[mid] == x) return true;
        else if (sortedNumbers[mid] > x) end = mid - 1;
        else start = mid + 1;
    }
    return false;
}
```

Snippet 1.7: Binary search. Source class name: BinarySearch.

 Go to `https://goo.gl/R9e31d` to access the code.

Take a look at the following diagram:

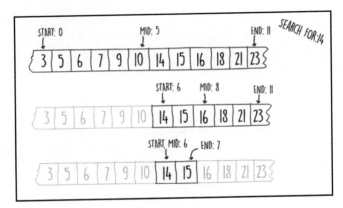

Figure 1.3: Binary search steps

Assuming the worst case scenario, how big would the input size have to be if our binary search algorithm is 95 array jumps (such as the one shown in *Figure 1.3*)? Since this is a binary search, where we're splitting the search space in two, we should use a logarithm of base 2.

Also, the inverse of a logarithm is the exponential. Thus, we can say the following:

- $log_2 n = 95$
- $2^{95} = n$
- $39614081257132168796771975168 = n$

For the record, 2^{95} is larger than the number of seconds in the universe by far. This example demonstrates how well these types of algorithm scale. Even for huge inputs, the number of steps performed stays very small.

Logarithmic algorithms are the opposite of exponential ones. As the input gets bigger, the rate of performance degradation gets smaller. This is a very desirable property as it means that our problem can scale to a huge size and would hardly affect our performance. In this section, we gave one such example of this class of complexity.

Exponential Complexity

As we have seen previously, algorithms that have an exponential runtime complexity scale really poorly. There are many examples of problems for which only an $O(k^n)$ solution is known. Improving these algorithms is a very dynamic area of study in computer science. Examples of these include the traveling salesman problem and cracking a password using a brute force approach. Now, let's see an example of such problem.

A prime number is only divisible by itself and one. The example problem we present here is called the **prime factorization problem**. It turns out that if you have the right set of prime numbers, you can create any other possible number by multiplying them all together. The problem is to find out these prime numbers. More specifically, given an integer input, find all the prime numbers that are factors of the input (primes that when multiplied together give us the input).

A lot of the current cryptographic techniques rely on the fact that no known polynomial time algorithm is known for prime factorization. However, nobody has yet proved that one doesn't exist. Hence, if a fast technique to find prime factors is ever discovered, many of the current encryption strategies will need to be reworked.

Snippet 1.8 shows one implementation for this problem, called **trail division**. If we take an input decimal number of n digits, this algorithm would perform in $O(10^n)$ in the worst case. The algorithm works by using a counter (called **factor** in *Snippet 1.8*) starting at two and checks whether if it's a factor of the input. This check is done by using the modulus operator. If the modulus operation leaves no remainder, then the value of the counter is a factor and is added to the factor list. The input is then divided by this factor. If the counter is not a factor (the mod operation leaves a remainder), then the counter is incremented by one. This continues until x is reduced to one. This is demonstrated by the following code snippet:

```
public List<Long> primeFactors(long x) {
    ArrayList<Long> result = new ArrayList<>();
    long factor = 2;
    while (x > 1) {
        if (x % factor == 0) {
            result.add(factor);
            x /= factor;
        } else {
            factor += 1;
        }
    }
    return result;
}
```

Snippet 1.8: Prime factors. Source class name: FindPrimeFactors.

 Go to `https://goo.gl/xU4HBV` to access the code.

Try executing the preceding code for the following two numbers:

- *2100078578*
- *2100078577*

Why does it take so long when you try the second number? What type of input triggers the worst-case runtime of this code?

The worst case of the algorithm is when the input is a prime number, wherein it needs to sequentially count all the way up to the prime number. This is what happens in the second input.

On the other hand, the largest prime factor for the first input is only 10,973, so the algorithm only needs to count up to this, which it can do quickly.

Exponential complexity algorithms are usually best avoided, and an alternate solution should be investigated. This is due to its really bad scaling with the input size. This is not to say that these types of algorithms are useless. They may be suitable if the input size is small enough or if it's guaranteed not to hit the worst case.

Constant Complexity

The efficiency of constant runtime algorithms remains fixed as we increase the input size. Many examples of these exist. Consider, for example, accessing an element in an array. Access performance doesn't depend on the size of the array, so as we increase the size of the array, the access speed stays constant.

Consider the code in *Snippet 1.9*. The number of operations performed remains constant, irrespective of the size of the input radius. Such an algorithm is said to have a runtime complexity of *O(1)*. The code snippet is as follows:

```
private double circleCircumference(int radius) {
    return 2.0 * Math.PI * radius;
}
```

Snippet 1.9: Circle circumference. Source class name: CircleOperations.

 Go to `https://goo.gl/Rp57PB` to access the code.

Constant complexity algorithms are the most desirable out of all the complexity classes for the best scaling. Many of the simple mathematical functions, such as finding the distance between two points and mapping a three-dimensional coordinate to a two-dimensional one, all fall under this class.

Activity: Developing a Faster Intersection Algorithm

Scenario

We have already seen an algorithm that produces an intersection between two input arrays in *Snippet 1.6*.

We have already shown how the runtime complexity of this algorithm is $O(n^2)$. Can we write an algorithm with a faster runtime complexity?

To find a solution for this problem, think about how you would you go about finding the intersection by hand between two decks of playing cards. Imagine you take a subset from each shuffled deck; which technique would you use to find the common cards between the first and second deck?

Aim

To improve the performance of the array intersection algorithm and reduce its runtime complexity.

Prerequisites

- Ensure that you have a class available at:
  `https://github.com/TrainingByPackt/Data-Structures-and-Algorithms-in-Java/blob/master/src/main/java/com/packt/datastructuresandalg/lesson1/activity/improveintersection/Intersection.java`
- You will find two methods for improving the intersection:
  - The slow intersection:

    ```
    public List<Integer> intersection(int[] a, int[] b)
    ```

  - The empty stub, returning null:

    ```
    public List<Integer> intersectionFast(int[] a, int[]
    b)
    ```

- Use the second, empty stub method, to implement a faster alternative for the intersection algorithm.
- Assume that each array has no duplicate values. If you have your project set up, you can run the unit test for this activity by running the following command:

    ```
    gradlew test --tests
    com.packt.datastructuresandalg.lesson1.activity.improveintersection
    *
    ```

Steps for Completion

1. Assume that we have a way to sort the inputs in $O(n \log n)$. This is provided in the following method:

```java
public void mergeSort(int[] input) {
   Arrays.sort(input);
}
```

We can use this method to sort one input array, or both, and make the intersection easier.

2. To sort one input array, we can use a binary search on it. The runtime complexity is $O(n \log n)$ for the merge sort plus $O(n \log n)$ for the binary search per item in the first list. This is $n \log + n \log n$ which results in a final $O(n \log n)$.

3. Sort both arrays, and have two pointers, one for each array.

4. Go through the input arrays in a linear fashion.

5. Advance a pointer if the other pointer is pointing to a larger value.

6. If the values at both pointers are equal, both pointers are incremented. The runtime complexity for this algorithm is $2 * (n \log n)$ for the two merge sorts plus the n for the linear pass after the sorting. This results in $2 * (n \log n) + n$ with a final $O(n \log n)$.

Summary

In this chapter, we gave an introduction to algorithmic complexity and the notation to describe it. We have shown you how big O notation can be used to describe how well an algorithm scales as the input gets bigger. We have also seen various examples of complexities and shown you how you can intuitively differentiate between them. Understanding big O notations comes in handy when you need to design and implement new solutions or when you are diagnosing performance issues.

Sorting Algorithms and Fundamental Data Structures

2

In the previous chapter, we saw how the intersection problem can be improved by using a sorting algorithm. This is common with many problems. If the data is organized in an ordered manner, a more efficient algorithm can be developed. In this chapter, we will start by exploring three types of sorting techniques, which are bubble, quick, and merge sorting. Later, we will learn different ways to organize data using fundamental data structures.

By the end of this chapter, you will be able to:

- Describe how bubble sorting works
- Implement faster sorting with quick sort
- Characterize merge sorting
- Build a linked list data structure
- Implement queues
- Describe the stack data structure

Introducing Bubble Sorting

Bubble sorting is the simplest sorting algorithm out there. The technique involves making multiple passes over the input array and swapping unordered elements close to one another. The technique is called bubble sort, as the sorted list "bubbles" up from the tail end of the list.

Understanding Bubble Sorting

All sorting algorithms accept a list of elements and return them ordered. The main difference between each algorithm is the manner in which the sorting is done. Bubble sorting works by swapping adjacent elements. This pushes the sorted elements toward the end of the list.

Snippet 2.1 shows the pseudocode for bubble sort. The algorithm involves three simple tasks, which involves repeatedly stepping through the list to sort, comparing adjacent elements, and swapping them around if the first element is bigger than the second.

How many passes do we need to perform on the array until our list is sorted? It turns out that to guarantee that our list is sorted, we need to do *(n - 1)* passes on the list, *n* being the length of our array. We will show why *(n - 1)* passes are needed in the next section, but this is the main reason why bubble sort has a runtime complexity of $O(n^2)$, since we're processing *n* elements for *n - 1* times.

The pseudocode for bubble sort is as follows:

```
bubbleSort(array)
  n = length(array)
  for (k = 1 until n)
    for (j = 0 until -1)
      if(array[j] > array[j + 1])
        swap(array, j, j + 1)
```

Snippet 2.1: Bubble sort pseudocode

 The swap function in the *Snippet 2.1* switches the values of the two array pointers j and j+1 using a temporary variable.

Implementing Bubble Sort

To implement bubble sort in Java, follow these steps:

1. Apply the pseudocode shown in *Snippet 2.1* in Java. Create a class and a method, accepting an array to sort as follows:

   ```
   public void sort(int[] numbers)
   ```

2. The slightly tricky part of this algorithm is the swapping logic. This is done by assigning one of the elements to be swapped to a temporary variable, as shown in *Snippet 2.2*:

```
public void sort(int[] numbers) {
    for (int i = 1; i < numbers.length; i++) {
        for (int j = 0; j < numbers.length - 1; j++) {
            if (numbers[j] > numbers[j + 1]) {
                int temp = numbers[j];
                numbers[j] = numbers[j + 1];
                numbers[j + 1] = temp;
            }
        }
    }
}
```

Snippet 2.2: Bubble sort solution. Source class name: BubbleSort

 Go to `https://goo.gl/7atHVR` to access the code.

Although bubble sort is very easy to implement, it's also one of the slowest sorting methods out there. In the next section, we will look at how we can slightly improve the performance of this algorithm.

Improving Bubble Sorting

There are two main techniques we can adopt to improve the performance of bubble sort. It's important to realize that although both of these strategies improve the overall performance of bubble sort in the average case; in the worst case, the algorithm still has the same poor runtime complexity of $O(n^2)$.

The first small enhancement we can make to the original bubble sort is to make use of the fact that a sorted "bubble" is building at the end of the list. With every pass we make, another item is added at the end portion of this bubble. This is the reason why $(n - 1)$ passes are needed.

This is also shown in *Figure 2.1*. In this diagram, the items shown in the dotted circle are already sorted in the correct place:

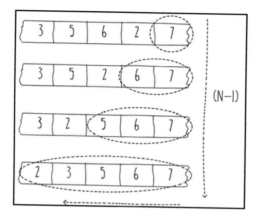

Figure 2.1: Bubble forming toward the end of the list

We can use this fact so we don't try to sort the elements inside this bubble. We can do this by slightly modifying our Java code, as shown in *Snippet 2.3*. In the inner loop, instead of processing until the end of the list, we can stop just before the sorted bubble, until `numbers.length - i`. For brevity, in *Snippet 2.3* we have replaced the swap logic with a method as follows:

```java
public void sortImprovement1(int[] numbers) {
    for (int i = 1; i < numbers.length; i++) {
        for (int j = 0; j < numbers.length - i; j++) {
            if (numbers[j] > numbers[j + 1]) {
                swap(numbers, j, j + 1);
            }
        }
    }
}
```

Snippet 2.3: Bubble sort improvement 1. Source class name: BubbleSort

 Go to `https://goo.gl/vj267K` to access the code.

If we give a sorted list to our bubble sort algorithm, we will still make multiple passes on it without modifying it. We can further improve the algorithm by cutting short the outer loop when the list inside the array is fully sorted. We can check that the array is sorted by checking if any swaps were done during our last pass. In this manner, if we give our method an already sorted list, we just need to do one pass on the array and leave it untouched. This means that the best case is now $O(n)$, although the worst case stays the same.

Implementing Bubble Sort Improvement

We need to improve the bubble sort algorithm by reducing the number of passes.

The steps to do this are as follows:

1. Change the bubble sort method so that it stops sorting if the array is untouched after an inner loop pass.
2. The solution can be developed easily if the outer for loop is changed into a `while` loop and a flag is kept to indicate if any elements have been swapped while going through the array. This is shown in the following code snippet:

```
public void sortImprovement2(int[] numbers) {
    int i = 0;
    boolean swapOccured = true;
    while (swapOccured) {
        swapOccured = false;
        i++;
        for (int j = 0; j < numbers.length - i; j++) {
            if (numbers[j] > numbers[j + 1]) {
                swap(numbers, j, j + 1);
                swapOccured = true;
            }
        }
    }
}
```

Snippet 2.4: Bubble sort improvement 2. Source class name: BubbleSort

Go to `https://goo.gl/HgVYfL` to access the code.

In this section, we have seen some simple tricks on how to improve the bubble sort algorithm. In the following sections, we shall look at some other sorting techniques that perform much faster than bubble sort.

Activity: Implementing Selection Sort in Java

Scenario

Selection sort is best understood by imagining that you have two lists, A and B. Initially, we have list A, containing all the unsorted elements, and list B is empty. The idea is to use B to store the sorted elements. The algorithm would work by finding the smallest element from A and moving it to the end of B. We keep on doing this until A is empty and B is full. Instead of using two separate lists, we can just use the same input array, but keeping a pointer to divide the array in two.

In real life, this can be explained by picturing how you would sort a deck of cards. Using a shuffled deck, you can go through the cards one by one until you find the lowest card. You set this aside as a new, second pile. You then look for the next-lowest card and once found, you put it at the bottom of the second pile. You repeat this until the first pile is empty.

One way to arrive at the solution is to first write the pseudocode that uses two arrays (A and B, in the preceding description). Then, adopt the pseudocode to store the sorted list (array B) in the same input array by using the swapping method.

Aim

Implement the selection sort in Java

Prerequisites

- Implement the sort method found in the following class, which is available on the GitHub repository for the book at the following path:
  ```
  https://github.com/TrainingByPackt/Data-Structures-and-Algorithms-in-
  Java/blob/master/src/main/java/com/packt/datastructuresandalg/lesson2/
  activity/selectionsort/SelectionSort.java
  ```
- The sort method should accept an integer array and sort it

 If you have your project set up, you can run the unit test for this activity by running the following command:
```
gradlew test --tests
com.packt.datastructuresandalg.lesson2.activity.selection
sort*
```

Steps for Completion

1. Split the input array in two by using an array index pointer
2. The `sort` method should accept an integer array and sort it
3. Iterate over the unsorted portion of the array to find the minimum
4. The minimum item is then swapped so that it can be added to the end of the sorted portion

Understanding Quick Sort

Quick sort is a big improvement over bubble sort. This sorting technique was developed by British computer scientist Tony Hoare. The algorithm works in three main steps:

1. Select a pivot
2. Partition the list so that elements on the left of the pivot are less than the value of the pivot and the ones on the right are greater
3. Repeat steps 1 and 2 on the left and right parts separately

Since recursion is required for quick sort, we will begin this section by giving an example of recursion. Later, we will see how the partitioning in the quick sort algorithm works, and in the end, we will put the recursion techniques to use in the final part.

Understanding Recursion

Recursion is a really useful tool for algorithm designers. It allows you to solve large problems by solving a smaller occurrence of the same problem. Recursive functions usually have a common structure with the following components:

- *One or more stopping conditions*: Under certain conditions, it would stop the function from calling itself again
- *One or more recursive calls*: This is when a function (or method) calls itself

In the next example, we will pick the binary search problem seen in the previous chapter and change the algorithm to work in a recursive manner. Consider the binary search problem discussed in `Chapter 1`, *Algorithms and Complexities*, listed in *Snippet 1.7*. The implementation is iterative, that is, it loops until an item is found or the `end` parameter is equal or greater than the `start` variable. The following code snippet shows pseudocode on how we can change this method into a recursive function:

```
binarySearch(x, array, start, end)
  if(start <= end)
    mid = (end - start) / 2 + start
    if (array[mid] == x) return true
    if (array[mid] > x) return binarySearch(x, array, start, mid - 1)
    return binarySearch(x, array, mid + 1, end)
  return false
```

Snippet 2.5: Recursive binary search pseudocode

There are actually two stopping conditions in a recursive binary search. The function stops the recursive chain if it either finds the search item at the midpoint or if the start array pointer is greater than the end, meaning the item wasn't found. The stopping condition can easily be found by examining any return paths that don't involve further recursive calls.

Implementing Binary Search Recursively

To implement binary search recursively in Java, we'll follow these steps:

1. Using the pseudocode shown in *Snippet 2.5*, implement a recursive binary search function.
2. Provide another method with a signature that only contains the search item and the sorted array as input. This method will then call the recursive function with appropriate values as follows:

```
public boolean binarySearch(int x, int[] sortedNumbers)
```

Output

The following code shows the additional method making the initial call and the recursive function as follows:

```
public boolean binarySearch(int x, int[] sortedNumbers, int start,
int end) {
  if (start <= end) {
    int mid = (end - start) / 2 + start;
```

```
      if (sortedNumbers[mid] == x) return true;
      if (sortedNumbers[mid] > x)
      return binarySearch(x, sortedNumbers, start, mid - 1);
      return binarySearch(x, sortedNumbers, mid + 1, end);
    }
  return false; }
```

Snippet 2.6: Recursive binary search. Source class name: BinarySearchRecursive

 Go to `https://goo.gl/pPaZVZ` to access the code.

Recursion is an essential tool for any developer and we'll make use of it in many parts in this book. In this section, we implemented an example for binary searching. In the next section, we shall look at how partitioning works in the quicksort algorithm.

Quicksort Partitioning

Partitioning is the process by which we reorder our array so that elements with a value less than our pivot are moved to the left of the pivot and those with a larger value are moved to the right (see *Figure 2.2*). There are numerous manners in which we can do this. Here, we will describe an easy-to-understand scheme known as **Lomuto Partitioning**.

Take a look at this diagram:

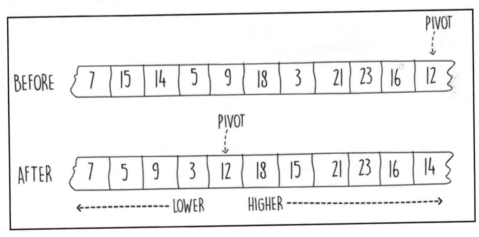

Figure 2.2: Before and after partitioning of an array

Many other schemes exist. The Lomuto scheme has the drawback that it is not very performant when it is used on already-sorted lists. The original Hoare partition scheme performs better and works by having the array processed from both ends. The original Hoare scheme performs better as it does fewer swaps, although it also suffers from slow performance when a sorted list is used as input. Both the Lomuto and Hoare schemes result in non-stable sorting. A stable sort means that if two or more elements have the same key value, they will appear in the same input order as the sorted output. There are other schemes that can be used to make quick sort stable, but they utilize more memory.

To get a good perception on this partitioning scheme, it is best to simplify what the algorithm is doing in five simple steps, as follows:

1. Pick the right most element of the array as the pivot.
2. Start from the left and find the next element that is larger than the pivot.
3. Swap this element with the next, which is smaller than pivot element.
4. Repeat steps 2 and 3 until no more swapping is possible.
5. Swap the first item which is larger than the pivot's value with the pivot itself.

To perform efficient partitioning using the steps mentioned, we can make use of two pointers, one pointing to the first item larger than the pivot value and the other used to search for the value that is smaller than pivot value.

In the following code, these are the integer pointers named x and i, respectively. The algorithm starts by choosing the pivot as the last item on the input array. It then processes the array from left to right in a single pass using the variable i. If the element currently being processed at i is smaller than the pivot, x is incremented and swapped. Using this technique, variable x is either pointing to a value larger than the pivot or the value of x is the same as i, in which case swapping will not modify the array. Once the loop exits, we perform the final step of swapping the first item that is larger than the pivot's value with the pivot. The code is as follows:

```
private int partition(int[] numbers, int start, int end) {
    int pivot = numbers[end];
    int x = start - 1;
    for (int i = start; i < end; i++) {
        if (numbers[i] < pivot) {
            x++;
            swap(numbers, x, i);
        }
    }
}
```

```
    swap(numbers, x + 1, end);
    return x + 1;
}
```

Snippet 2.7: Partitioning for quick sort. Source class name: QuickSort

 Go to `https://goo.gl/vrStai` to access the code.

Activity: Understanding the Partitioning Method

Scenario

To better understand the partitioning method used in *Snippet 2.7*, walk through it one step at a time using an example.

Aim

To understand how the Lomuto partitioning works.

Steps for completion

1. Dry run the code mentioned in *Snippet 2.7* for each element in the array by incrementing the values of variables x and i.
2. Complete the following table, assuming that the pivot is the last element of the list, that is, 16:

i	Array	x
–	[4, 5, 33, 17, 3, 21, 1, 16]	−1
0	[4, 5, 33, 17, 3, 21, 1, 16]	0
1		
2	[4, 5, 33, 17, 3, 21, 1, 16]	1
3		
4	[4, 5, 3, 17, 33, 21, 1, 16]	2
5		
6		
7		
final	[4, 5, 3, 1, 16, 21, 17, 33]	3

Table 2.1: Steps through the partitioning method

In this section, we have gained an understanding of how partitioning in quick sort works. In the next section, we'll put the partitioning method to use by including it in the full quick sort algorithm.

Putting It All Together

The quick sort is from a class of algorithms called divide and conquer. We will see many other examples from this class in the book, and we will go into detail on divide and conquer in Chapter 4, *Algorithm Design Paradigms*. For now, it's important to know that divide and conquer algorithms keep on splitting the problem into smaller ones until the problem is small enough that it becomes trivial to solve. This splitting can be easily implemented using recursion.

In quick sorting, we keep on recursively partitioning the array in this manner until the problem is small enough that we can easily solve it. When the array has only one element, the solution is simple: the array stays exactly as it is, as there is nothing to sort. This is the stopping condition of our recursive algorithm. When the array is larger than one element, we can keep dividing our array and use the partitioning method we developed in the previous section.

 There is also a non-recursive quick sort algorithm which makes use of a stack data structure, although it is a bit more complex to write. We will discuss stacks and lists later on in this chapter.

The following code snippet shows the pseudocode for the complete quick sort. Just like most recursive functions, the code starts by checking the stopping condition. In this case, we check if the array has at least two elements by ensuring that the start array pointer is less than the end. The pseudocode is as follows:

```
quickSort(array, start, end)
  if(start < end)
    p = partition(array, start, end)
    quickSort(array, start, p - 1)
    quickSort(array, p + 1, end)
```

Snippet 2.8: Recursive quick sort pseudocode

When we have at least two elements in the array, we call the partitioning method. Then, using the pivot's last position (returned by the partitioning method), we recursively quick sort the left part and then the right part.

This is done by calling the same quick sort code using pointers of (start, p - 1) and (p + 1, end), not including the p, which is the pivot's position.

The trick to understanding how quick sort works is to realize that once we perform the partition call on the array, the element at the returned position (the pivot) doesn't need to move within the array anymore. This is because all the elements on its right are larger and the ones on the left are smaller, so the pivot is in the correct final position.

Implementing Quick Sort

To implement quick sort in Java, follow these steps:

1. Implement the pseudocode shown in *Snippet 2.8* in Java, calling the partitioning method shown in *Snippet 2.7*.
2. The following code shows the recursive implementation in Java, making use of the partition method developed in the preceding section:

```java
private void sort(int[] numbers, int start, int end) {
    if (start < end) {
        int p = partition(numbers, start, end);
        sort(numbers, start, p - 1);
        sort(numbers, p + 1, end);
    }
}
```

Snippet 2.9: Solution for quick sort. Source class name: Quicksort

In this section, we have described the quick sort algorithm, which is much faster than the bubble sort algorithm that we saw in the previous section. On average, this algorithm performs in $O(n \log n)$, a huge improvement over bubble sort's $O(n^2)$. However, in the worst case, the algorithm still performs in $O(n^2)$. The worst-case input of quick sort depends on the type of partitioning scheme in use. In the Lomuto scheme discussed in this section, the worst case occurs when the input is already sorted. In the next section, we will examine another sorting algorithm for which the worst runtime case is $O(n \log n)$.

Using Merge Sort

Although the quicksort on average is pretty fast, it still has the theoretical worst time complexity of $O(n^2)$. In this section, we shall examine another sorting algorithm, called **merge sort**, in which the worst time complexity is $O(n \log n)$. Similar to quick sort, merge sort belongs to the divide and conquer class of algorithms.

Merge sort can be summarized in three simple steps as follows:

1. Split the array in the middle
2. Recursively sort each part separately
3. Merge the two sorted parts together

In the following section, we will develop the preceding steps gradually, at each turn slowly building our understanding of how merge sorting works.

 Although merge sort is theoretically faster than quick sort, in practice, some implementations of quick sort can be more efficient than merge sort. Additionally, the merge sort uses about $O(n)$ memory as opposed to quick sort, which is $O(log\ n)$.

Dividing the Problem

In the preceding section, we saw how we can use a recursive technique to split the problem into smaller multiple ones until the solution becomes easy to solve. Merge sort uses the same approach. The base case for our recursive technique is the same as quick sort. This is when the array is only one element long. When the array to sort only contains one item, the array is already sorted.

Figure 2.3 shows how merge sort array splitting occurs. At each step, we find the midpoint of the array and split the array in two. We then recursively sort the left and right part of the split array separately. We can stop the recursive call once the total elements to sort is equal to one as shown in the following figure:

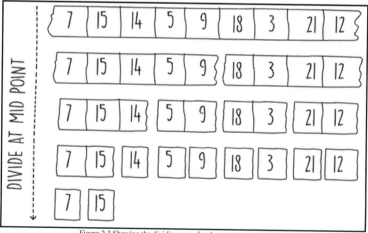

Figure 2.3 Showing the dividing steps for the merge sort algorithm

Implementing Merge Sort

We need to complete the pseudocode for a merge sort algorithm.

Keeping in mind that the merge sort's recursive part is very similar to the quick sort algorithm we saw in the preceding section, complete the pseudocode shown in the following code as follows:

```
mergeSort(array, start, end)
    if(_____)
       midPoint = _____
       mergeSort(array, _____, _____)
       mergeSort(array, _____, _____)
       merge(array, start, midPoint, end)
```

Snippet 2.10: Recursive merge sort pseudocode exercise

The pseudocode for merge sort can be completed as follows:

```
mergeSort(array, start, end)
   if(start < end)
       midPoint = (end - start) / 2 + start
       mergeSort(array, start, midPoint)
       mergeSort(array, midPoint + 1, start)
       merge(array, start, midPoint, end)
```

Snippet 2.11: Recursive merge sort pseudocode solution

The merge sort algorithm is from the same class of algorithms as quick sort; however, its runtime and space complexity are different. Instead of dividing the array from the pivot's position, the merge sort always partitions the array at the midpoint. This is a similar process to binary search and results in $log_2 n$ array divisions. In the next section, we will introduce the merge part of the merge sort algorithm, where the two different parts of the split array are combined into a sorted one.

Merging the Problem

How do you merge two sorted lists into a sorted one? This is the task of the `merge()` function, which is found at the end of the pseudocode shown in the preceding section. This process is shown in *Figure 2.4*. Merging two sorted lists is an easier task than sorting from scratch.

This is similar to the intersection problem we saw in `Chapter 1`, *Algorithms and Complexities*.

We can merge in linear time utilizing just two pointers and an empty array as shown in the following diagram:

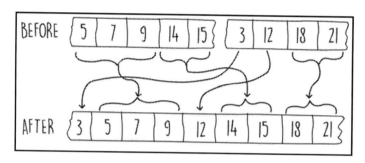

Figure 2.4: Before and after merging two sorted arrays

 Since the two parts of the split array are both sorted, it's easy to merge the two together. A useful analogy is to refer back to how the intersection problem we saw in `Chapter 1`, *Algorithms and Complexities*, got a lot easier once the input arrays were both sorted. A similar algorithm can be used here.

The pseudocode for the merging is shown in the following code snippet. In this code, the `copyArray()` function simply takes in a source array as a first argument and copies it to the target array, that is, the second argument. It makes use of the `start` variable as a pointer, indicating where to place the first element of the source array onto the target one. The pseudocode is as follows:

```
merge(array, start, middle, end)
  i = start
  j = middle + 1
  arrayTemp = initArrayOfSize(end - start + 1)
  for (k = 0 until end-start)
    if (i <= middle && (j > end || array[i] <= array[j]))
      arrayTemp[k] = array[i]
      i++
    else
      arrayTemp[k] = array[j]
      j++
  copyArray(arrayTemp, array, start)
```

Snippet 2.12: Merge pseudocode for the merge sort

In the merging part of the merge sort, we create a temporary array which is of size equal to the size of two array parts together. We then do a single pass on this array, filling the temporary array one item at a time by picking the smallest item between the two input lists (represented by the start, middle, and end pointers). After picking an item from one of the lists, we advance the pointer of that list and repeat until the merge is complete.

There are various Java tools we can use to implement the `copyArray()` function shown at the end of *Snippet 2.12*. We can simply implement a `for` loop and implement the `copy()` function ourselves. Alternatively, we can make use of Java's streams and write the copy in a single line. Possibly the easiest manner is to make use of the `System.arrayCopy()` function.

Merge sort is theoretically one of the fastest sorting algorithms. The drawback of its speed is that it consumes a bit more memory, although some implementations exist that perform the merge step in place to save memory.

For comparison, we present multiple sorting techniques with their runtime and memory performances in the following table:

Algorithm name	Average case	Worst case	Memory	Stability
Bubble	$O(n^2)$	$O(n^2)$	$O(1)$	Stable
Selection	$O(n^2)$	$O(n^2)$	$O(1)$	Unstable
Insertion	$O(n^2)$	$O(n^2)$	$O(1)$	Stable
Quick	$O(n \log n)$	$O(n^2)$	$O(1)$	Unstable
Merge	$O(n \log n)$	$O(n \log n)$	$O(n)$	Stable
Heap	$O(n \log n)$	$O(n \log n)$	$O(1)$	Unstable

Table 2.2: Sorting algorithms

Activity: Implementing Merge Sort in Java

Scenario

Merge sorting is one of the fastest sorting techniques. It is used in many bundled libraries and APIs. In this activity, we will write an algorithm in Java to sort an array using merge sort.

Aim

To use the pseudocode shown in this section to implement the full merge sort algorithm in Java.

Prerequisites

To solve this activity, you have to implement the methods found in the following class, which is available on the GitHub repository for the book at the following path:

```
https://github.com/TrainingByPackt/Data-Structures-and-Algorithms-in-Java/blob/
master/src/main/java/com/packt/datastructuresandalg/lesson2/activity/mergesort/
MergeSort.java
```

 If you have your project set up, you can run the unit test for this activity by running the following command:
```
gradlew test --tests
com.packt.datastructuresandalg.lesson2.activity.mergesort
*
```

Steps for Completion

1. Start from the `mergeSort` method, which splits the array in two, recursively sorts both, and merges the result
2. Then, implement the merge method, which merges both ends of the split array into another space
3. After the merge is done, copy the new array back in place of the input array

Getting Started with Fundamental Data Structures

Data structures are a way to organize data so that it is efficiently accessible for the problem you are trying to solve. Choosing the right data structure will depend on the type of problem you're trying to solve (dictating the manner you access your data), the amount of data you need to organize, and the medium you use to store your data (memory, disk, and so on).

We have already seen and used one example of a data structure. In the preceding sections, we have made extensive use of arrays. Arrays are the most primitive of data structures. They provide access to your data using an index and are fixed in size (also called static). This is opposed to other dynamic data structures that can grow and make more space for data whenever it's needed.

Introducing Data Structures

More formally, a data structure is an organization of data elements, a collection of functions that can be applied on the data (such as add, delete, and search) and any relations between the different data elements. The following table shows common operations that some data structures provide:

Operation	Type	Description
search(key)	Non-modifying	An operation that, given the key to a particular value, will return the value stored in the data structure if it can be found.
side()	Non-modifying	The total number of values stored in the data structure.
add(value)	Modifying	Inserts a value in the data structure.
update(key, value)	Modifying	Updates an existing entry using the provided key and value.
delete(value)	Modifying	Removes an item of data from the data structure.
minimum()	Non-modifying	An operation supported only by ordered data structures, which will return the value with the minimal key.
maximum()	Non-modifying	An operation supported only by ordered data structures, which will return the value with the minimal key.

Table 2.3: Some common operations on data structures

In this section, we will see various types of dynamic data structures. We will start with linked lists, which are optimized for dynamic growth but are slow while searching. Then, we'll use these linked lists to implement other data structures on top, such as queues and stacks.

Linked Lists Structure

A linked list is a list of data items where each item only knows about the next item in the list if there is one. *Figure 2.5* shows one such example. Each box in the figure represents a container for a data item we need to store. This container, called a node, contains our data values and a pointer to the next node in the list. As the diagram shows, the node on the front of the list is called the head of the list and the last item of the list is called the tail.

Separate pointers to these nodes are stored for easy access of the data structure:

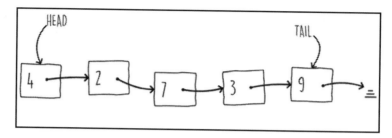

Figure 2.5: Linked list example

The advantage of using a linked list as opposed to an array is that a linked list can grow dynamically. When using an array, you allocate space in the start and that space remains fixed. If you allocate too much and the space remains unused, you're wasting resources. On the other hand, if you make your array too small, the data might not ft. In a linked list, however, the space is not fixed. The structure grows dynamically as you add more data and it shrinks, freeing memory space as you remove it.

Using an object-oriented language, such as Java, let's model the linked list using separate node instances that are connected together to build our linked list. The following code shows how we can model a linked list node in a Java class.

The class contains a self-reference so we can link multiple nodes in list fashion, as shown in the *Figure 2.5*.

```
public class LinkedListNode<V> {
  private V value;
  private LinkedListNode<V> next;
  public LinkedListNode(V value, LinkedListNode<V> next) {
    this.value = value;
    this.next = next;
  }
  public Optional<LinkedListNode<V>> getNext() {
    return Optional.ofNullable(next);
  }
}
```

Snippet 2.13: Linked list node class, with getters and setters omitted for brevity. Source class name: Linkedlistnode

 Go to `https://goo.gl/SAefic` to access the code.

Notice how we use Java's optional classes (instead of returning null pointers) to represent whether there is a link to the next node. The tail node of a linked list will always have an empty optional. We also make use of generics to model the type of data we want to store. This way, we can keep the structure as general as possible so that it can used by any data type.

The `Optional` class was introduced in Java 8 to give the ability to represent optional values instead of using nulls.

Converting the Linked List to a Doubly Linked List Structure

We need to modify the Java node class to support the doubly linked list structure.

A doubly linked list is a linked list in which each node contains a relation to the following and previous nodes. Modify the preceding code in *Snippet 2.13* to support this.

The following code shows the solution to this:

```
public class DblLinkedListNode<V> {
  private V value;
  private DblLinkedListNode<V> next;
  private DblLinkedListNode<V> previous;
  public DblLinkedListNode(V value,
  DblLinkedListNode<V> next,
  DblLinkedListNode<V> previous) {
    this.value = value;
    this.next = next;
    this.previous = previous;
  }
}
```

Snippet 2.14: Doubly linked list node class, with getters and setters omitted for brevity. Source class name: Dbllinkedlistnode

Go to `https://goo.gl/oJDQ8g` to access the code.
In a doubly linked list, the head node will have a null previous pointer while the tail node will have a null next pointer.

In this section, we saw how to model a linked list node using classes, generics, and optional references. In the next section, we shall see how to implement some of the linked list operations.

Linked Lists Operations

Before we can use any linked list operations, we need to initialize the data structure and mark it as empty. Conceptually, this is when the head of the list is pointing to nothing. We can do this in Java by adding this logic in a constructor.

The following code snippet shows this. Notice that, once again, we use generics to hold the type of the items we want to store in the linked list:

```
public class LinkedList<V> {
  private LinkedListNode<V> head;
  public LinkedList() {
    head = null;
  }
}
```

Snippet 2.15: Initializing the linked list data structure using constructors. Source class name: Linkedlist

 Go to `https://goo.gl/vxpkRt` to access the code.

How can we add and remove items from the head of the list? Adding a node in a linked list requires a two pointer reassignment. On the new node, you set the next pointer to point to whatever the head pointer is assigned to. Then, you set the head pointer to point to this newly created node. This process is shown in *Figure 2.6*. Deleting from the front of the list is the reverse. You set the head pointer to point to the next pointer of the node at the old head. For completeness, you can set this next pointer to point to nothing:

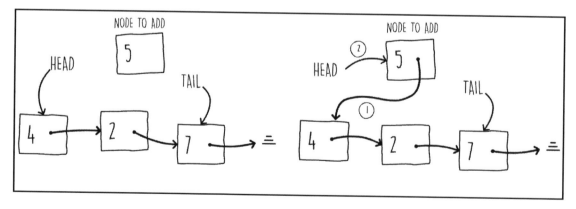

Figure 2.6: Adding a node to the front of the list

To locate an item in a list, we need to traverse the entire list until we find the item we're searching or reach the end of the list. This can be done easily by starting at the head pointer and always following the node's next pointer until you either find the node with the value you're looking for or you run out of nodes. For example, the next pointer is a null one.

The following code *snippet* shows the addFront() and deleteFront() operations for a linked list. For the addFront() method, we simply create a new node with its next pointer set as the current head pointer. Then, we assign the head to the new node. Notice in the delete method how we make use of Java's Optional objects. If the head pointer is null, it will stay null and we don't change anything. Otherwise, we flatten it to the next pointer. Finally, we set the first node's next pointer as null. This last step is not necessary since the orphaned node will be garbage collected; however, we're including it for completeness.

The code is as follows:

```
public void addFront(V item) {
    this.head = new LinkedListNode<>(item, head);
}
public void deleteFront() {
    Optional<LinkedListNode<V>> firstNode = Optional.
    ofNullable(this.head);
    this.head = firstNode.flatMap(LinkedListNode::getNext).
    orElse(null);
    firstNode.ifPresent(n -> n.setNext(null));
}
```

Snippet 2.16: Adding and deleting from the front of the linked list. Source class name: Linkedlist

Go to https://goo.gl/D5NAoT to access the code.

The following code snippet shows one way to implement a find method. Again, observe how we make use of Java's `Optional` methods. We start a `while` loop from the head pointer and keep on moving to the next node as long as there is a node present and that node doesn't contain the item we're looking for. We then return the last pointer, which can be an empty optional or a node containing a match:

```
public Optional<LinkedListNode<V>> find(V item) {
    Optional<LinkedListNode<V>> node = Optional.ofNullable(this.head);

    while (node.filter(n -> n.getValue() != item).isPresent()) {
        node = node.flatMap(LinkedListNode::getNext);
    }
    return node;
}
```

Snippet 2.17: Adding and deleting from the front of the linked list. Source class name: Linkedlist

 Go to `https://goo.gl/6pQm3T` to access the code. The `find()` method on a linked list has the worst runtime complexity of *O(n)*. This happens when either the matching item is at the end of the list or the item is not in the list at all.

In the preceding example, we have shown how to add an item at the head of the list. How can we insert this into a linked list at an arbitrary point? *Figure 2.7* shows how we can do this in two steps:

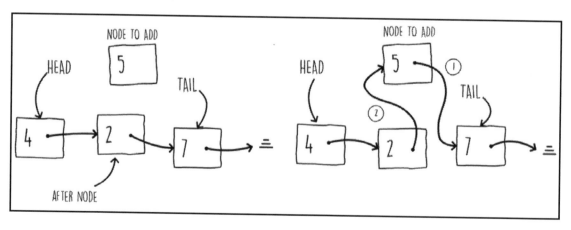

Figure 2.7: Adding a node at an arbitrary position in the list

Snippet 2.18 shows how we can do this. It is a Java method called `addAfter()` accepting a node and an item to insert. The method adds a node, containing the item, after the `aNode` argument. The implementation follows the steps shown in *Figure 2.7*.

```java
public void addAfter(LinkedListNode<V> aNode, V item) {
    aNode.setNext(new LinkedListNode<>(item, aNode.getNext().orElse(null)));
}
```

Snippet 2.18: Solution method for addAfter operation. Source class name: Linkedlist

Go to `https://goo.gl/Sjxc6T` to access this code.

Activity: Traversing the Linked List

Scenario

We have a linked list containing some elements and we need to build a string of the form `[3,6,4,2,4]`. If the list is empty, it should output `[]`.

Aim

To write code in Java for traversing the linked list.

Steps for Completion

1. Write a `toString()` method in the `LinkedList` class as follows:

   ```java
   public String toString() {
   }
   ```

2. Use a `while` loop to traverse the linked list.

In this section, we have seen how we can implement the various operations found in the linked list. The data structure will be a base tool that we will use to model queues and stacks. Linked lists will also be extensively used in more advanced algorithms further along the book.

Queues

Queues are abstract data structures that are meant to emulate the workings of real life queues. They are used extensively in various applications, such resource allocation, scheduling, sorting, and many others. They are typically implemented using a double linked list, although many other implementations exists. A queue usually consists of two operations; an enqueue operation, where items are added to the rear of the queue, and an opposite dequeue operation, where items are removed from the front of the queue. These two operations make the mode of operation of this data structure **First In First Out** (**FIFO**).

We can implement an efficient queue using a double linked list. This enables us implement the dequeue operation by removing an item from the head of the linked list. enqueue is simply adding an item to the tail of the linked list. *Figure 2.8* shows how the two operations are performed:

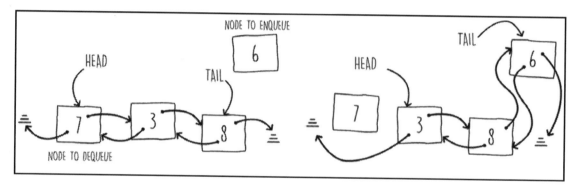

Figure 2.8: Enqueuing and dequeuing using a double linked list

To dequeue an item using a double linked list as a base data structure, we just need to move the head to the next item in the list and unlink the old head by pointing the previous pointer to nothing. Enqueuing at the tail is a three-step process. Point the new node's preceding pointer to the current tail, then point the current tail's next pointer to the new node, and finally moving the tail to the new node. The pseudocode for both of these operations is shown in the following code snippet:

```
dequeue(head)
   if (head != null)
     node = head
     head = head.next
     if (head != null) head.previous = null
     return node.value
   return null
enqueue(tail, item)
```

```
node = new Node(item)
node.previous = tail
if (tail != null) tail.next = node
if (head == null) head = node
tail = node
```

Snippet 2.19: Enqueuing and dequeuing using a doubly linked list

Adding and Deleting the Elements from the Queue

To implement the enqueue() and dequeue() methods in Java, follow these steps:

1. Using a double linked list, implement the dequeue and enqueue pseudocode shown in the preceding code in Java. Follow the structure and method signature shown in the following code snippet:

```
public class Queue<V> {
    private DblLinkedListNode<V> head;
    private DblLinkedListNode<V> tail;
    public void enqueue(V item)
    public Optional<V> dequeue()
}
```

Snippet 2.20: Exercise class structure and method signatures

2. The enqueue() method can be implemented as shown in the following code:

```
public void enqueue(V item) {
    DblLinkedListNode<V> node = new DblLinkedListNode<>(item, null,
tail);
    Optional.ofNullable(tail).ifPresent(n -> n.setNext(node));
    tail = node;
    if(head == null) head = node;
}
```

Snippet 2.21: Exercise class structure and method signatures. Source class name: Queue

 Go to https://goo.gl/FddeYu to access the code for dequeue() method.

Queues are dynamic data structures that have a FIFO ordering. In the next section, we shall explore another data structure with a different ordering called a stack.

Stacks

Stacks, typically also implemented using linked lists, work differently than queues. Instead of the FIFO ordering, they have a **Last In First Out (LIFO)** ordering (see *Figure 2.9*). They have two main operations called push, which adds an item on top of the stack, and pop, which removes and returns one item from the top of the stack. Like queues, stacks are heavily used in many algorithms, such as depth first search traversal, expression evaluations, and many others:

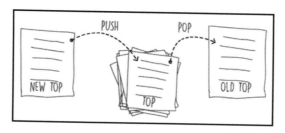

Figure 2.9: Pushing and popping operations on a stack of papers

To model a stack, it's enough to use a simple linked list. The head of the linked list can be used to reference the top of the stack. Every time we need to push something on the top of our stack, we can use the addFront() method we developed in the preceding sections. The implementations differ only in the fact that the pop operation returns the optional item on the top of the stack. Both push and pop can been seen in the Java implementation in the following code snippet. Notice how the pop operations return an optional value which is populated if the stack is not empty.

A one-way linked list is enough to model a stack since we only need to operate from one end of the list. For a queue, we needed to modify both the head and tail of the linked list, hence it was more efficient to use a double linked list. The following code shows the implementation of the push() and pop() methods:

```java
public void push(V item) {
   head = new LinkedListNode<V>(item, head);
}
public Optional<V> pop() {
   Optional<LinkedListNode<V>> node = Optional.ofNullable(head);
   head = node.flatMap(LinkedListNode::getNext).orElse(null);
   return node.map(LinkedListNode::getValue);
}
```

Snippet 2.22: Push and pop operations in java. Source class name: Stack

Go to `https://goo.gl/uUhuqg` to access the code.

Reversing a String

We need to make use of a stack data structure for reversing a string.

Follow these steps:

1. To reverse the string, push of each character of the input string and then pop everything out, one at a time, building a reversed string. The method signature can be as follows:

   ```
   public String reverse(String str)
   ```

2. The following code shows how a string can be reversed using the stack data structure:

   ```java
   public String reverse(String str) {
       StringBuilder result = new StringBuilder();
       Stack<Character> stack = new Stack<>();
       for (char c : str.toCharArray())
       stack.push(c);
       Optional<Character> optChar = stack.pop();
       while (optChar.isPresent()) {
           result.append(optChar.get());
           optChar = stack.pop();
       }
       return result.toString();
   }
   ```

   Snippet 2.23: Reverse a string solution Source class name: StringReverse

 Go to `https://goo.gl/UN2d5U` to access the code.

Stack data structures are extensively used in computer science for many algorithms. In this section, we have seen how to implement them in a dynamic fashion using linked lists. In the next section, we shall see how to model stacks and queue in a static manner using arrays.

Modeling Stacks and Queues Using Arrays

Stacks and queues don't necessarily need to be dynamic. You may want a more concise implementation if you know your data requirements are of a fixed size. Using an array approach to model stacks and queues guarantees that your data structure will only grow up to a certain size. The other advantage of using an array is that the array approach is more memory efficient if you can live with having a static data structure. The catch with static data structures is that the queue or stack can only grow to a maximum fixed size of your initially allocated array.

Implementing a stack using an array involves first initializing an empty array with a fixed size. Then, it's a matter of keeping an index pointer to the top of the stack, initially pointing to zero. As we push items on the stack, we place the item at this index and increment the pointer by one. When we need to pop an element, we reduce this pointer by one and read the value. This process is shown in the following code:

```
public StackArray(int capacity) {
  array = (V[]) new Object[capacity];
}
public void push(V item) {
  array[headPtr++] = item;
}
public Optional<V> pop() {
  if (headPtr > 0) return Optional.of(array[--headPtr]);
  else return Optional.empty();
}
```

Snippet 2.24: Stack using an array instead of linked list. Source class name: Stackarray

 Go to `https://goo.gl/T61L33` to access the code

Implementing a queue using an array requires a little more thinking. The difficulty with a queue is that the structure is modified from both ends since it grows from the tail and shrinks from the head.

As we enqueue and dequeue the contents of the queue, it seems to be moving towards the right of the array. We need to deal with what happens when the contents reaches the end of our array. To make the queue work in an array, we just need to let our data wrap around the edges (think *Pacman, Figure 2.10*):

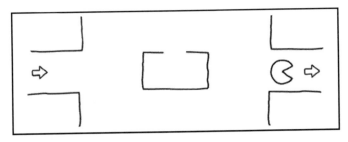

Figure 2.10: Array wrap around analogy

When we reach the end of our array, we can just start again from the beginning index. This wrap around mechanism is called a **circular buffer**. It can be implemented using the modulus operator to access any element in the underlying array. The following code snippet shows how this works. Notice that when we enqueue an item, we place it at the tail position and increment the tail pointer using the mod operator. When the pointer is larger or equal to the size of the array, it wraps around and starts again from zero. The same happens on the dequeue method, where we access and increment the head pointer in a similar fashion. The following code demonstrates it:

The implementation in *Snippet 2.25* does not check if the circular buffer is full before enqueuing another item. Implementing this check is given as an exercise in the next section.

```java
public void enqueue(V item) {
   array[tailPtr] = item;
   tailPtr = (tailPtr + 1) % array.length;
}
public Optional<V> dequeue() {
   if (headPtr != tailPtr) {
     Optional<V> item = Optional.of(array[headPtr]);
     headPtr = (headPtr + 1) % array.length;
     return item;
   } else return Optional.empty();
}
```

Snippet 2.25: Enqueue and dequeue using an array. Source class name: QueueArray

Go to `https://goo.gl/LJuYz9` to access this code.

Safe Enqueuing in an Array

We need to write a safe `enqueue()` method that will fail when the queue is full.

Steps for completion:

1. Modify the enqueue and dequeue methods shown in the preceding code so that the enqueue returns a Boolean value which is `false` when the queue is full and cannot accept further elements.

2. Implement the method signatures as follows:

```
public boolean enqueueSafe(V item)
public Optional<V> dequeueSafe()
```

3. The following *Snippet 2.26* provides an implementation of the `enqueueSafe()` method, returning a Boolean value when the queue is full:

```
private boolean full = false;
public boolean enqueueSafe(V item) {
  if (!full) {
    array[tailPtr] = item;
    tailPtr = (tailPtr + 1) % array.length;
    this.full = tailPtr == headPtr;
    return true;
  }
  return false;
}
```

Snippet 2.26: Safe Enqueue and dequeue solution. Source class name: QueueArray

Go to `https://goo.gl/cBszQL` to access the code for implementation of `dequeueSafe()` method.

We have seen how both queues and stacks can be implemented using a static array structure instead of using the dynamic linked list. This has the advantage of consuming less memory per element as a linked list has to store pointers to other nodes. However, this comes at the cost of having a limit on the structure size.

Activity: Evaluating the Postfix Expression

Scenario

We are used to writing mathematical expressions in the form of *1 + 2 * 3*. This type of notation is called an **infix**. Using infix notation, an operator is always in between two operators. There is a different notation called postfix, where the operator is after the operands. Examples of such expressions are shown in the following table:

Infix expression	Postfix expression
1 + 2	1 2 +
1 + 2 * 3	1 2 3 * +
(1 + 2) * 3	1 2 + 3 *
5 + 4 / 2 * 3	5 4 2 / 3 * +

Aim

Implement an algorithm that accepts a postfix string, evaluates it, and returns the result.

Prerequisites

- Implement the following method in the class which is available on the GitHub repository for the book at the following path:

  `https://github.com/TrainingByPackt/Data-Structures-and-Algorithms-in-Java/blob/master/src/main/java/com/packt/datastructuresandalg/lesson2/activity/postfix/EvalPostfix.java`

  ```
  public double evaluate(String postfix)
  ```

- Assume the operator and operands are always separated by a space, such as "5 2 +". The input string will look like the examples shown in the preceding table.

If you have your project set up, you can run the unit test for this activity by running the following command:

```
gradlew test --tests
com.packt.datastructuresandalg.lesson2.activity.postfix*
```

The solution becomes a lot simpler if you use one of the data structures we studied in this section.

Steps for Completion

1. Use the stack data structure to solve this problem
2. Start processing the expression from left to right
3. If you encounter a numeric operand, push it on the stack
4. If you encounter an operator, pop two items from the stack and perform the operation accordingly (addition, subtraction, and so on) and push the result back on the stack
5. Once you have processed the entire expression, the result should be the on the top of the stack

Summary

In this chapter, we laid the foundations for the more complex upcoming sections. In the first few sections, we saw how a simple problem such as sorting can have many solutions, all with different performance properties. We explored three main implementations, which were bubble, quick, and merge sort.

In later sections, we introduced data structures and studied various implementations and use cases of linked lists, queues, and stacks. We also saw how some data structures can be used as building blocks to build more complex ones on top. In the next chapter, we will study hash tables and binary trees, two important and widely used data structures.

Hash Tables and Binary Search Trees

3

In the preceding chapter, we introduced the concept of data structures by looking at arrays, linked lists, queues, and stacks. In this chapter, we will use some of these primitive structures to build more complex ones. We'll start the chapter by looking at hash tables, which are useful data structures for fast key-value lookup. In the second part of the chapter, we will learn about a more complex data structure that supports range queries, called binary trees.

By the end of this chapter, you will be able to:

- Describe how hash tables work
- Implement two main techniques to deal with hash collisions
- Characterize different hashing choices
- Explain the terminology, structure, and operations of binary trees
- Demonstrate various tree traversal techniques
- Define balanced binary search trees

Introducing Hash Tables

A data structure that gives us the ability to insert, search, and optionally delete elements in a collection is called a **data dictionary**. Commonly, the type of data used is a key-value pair association, where we insert the key-value pair but search using a key to obtain the value.

Hash tables provide us with a fast data structure for organizing these key value pairs and implementing our data dictionary. They are useful in a wide variety of applications due to the quick lookup and ease of use for in-memory data storage. Insertion and search operations have a typical average runtime complexity of $O(1)$.

Understanding Hash Tables

Let's look at an example problem to help us understand the need for hash tables. Imagine you are a teacher, instructing a class of a maximum capacity of 30 students. The students sit at their assigned desks every day. To make your life easier, you decide to assign a sequential number from one to 30 to each desk. You then use this number to identify each student, and use your self-developed app to bring up the student's records after you enter the desk number (see *Figure 3.1*). This way, you can quickly look up details such as the student's name, date of birth, notes, and exam history:

Figure 3.1: App for displaying student's records for student at desk number eight

In this problem, a simple array can be used to store all students' records in memory. Each of the array's positions can contain one student record. This would allow you to access the array directly using a strategy of *index = deskNumber - 1*. If, in a particular year you have fewer students, and not all the desks are occupied, you will place nulls at the corresponding array index. This solution is shown in *Figure 3.2*.

This is an example of direct addressing, where each student's record is accessed using a key (the desk number). This type of solution can only be used when the possible key range is small enough to fit in an array which is directly in memory:

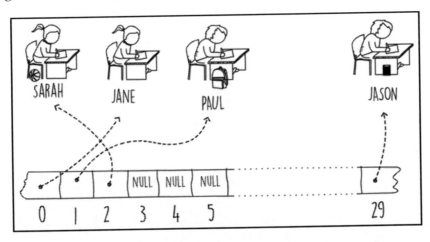

Figure 3.2: Example of direct addressing

To help us determine how efficiently we are using memory, we can measure the load factor. The load factor is simply a metric showing how fully utilized our data structure is. When the class is at max capacity, all the elements in the array will contain a record. We say that the load factor of our data structure is 1 (or at 100%). If, for example, only 15 students out of 30 spaces have registered for a particular year, the load factor is 0.5 (50%). A lower load factor value means that we are under-utilizing and wasting memory.

Now, let's expand our example to include not just a class but an entire school, and instead of teaching one class, you have now been promoted to the head of the entire school. In this new position, you want to keep student records for every person currently enrolled. You also want to store historical records for any past students that are no longer in the school. You decide to use the national ID or passport number as a key to uniquely identify each one of your students. Assuming this is a US or an EU school, the national ID or passport number typically consists of nine numeric digits or more.

Since our input range is quite big, directly addressing this would be very impractical.

Since the US passport number (or national ID) is typically nine numeric digits, we would have to construct a huge array to store any possible number. For a nine-digit numeric range, the array's size would be 1,000,000,000. Assuming each pointer is four bytes, this array alone would consume almost 4 GB! The load factor of this example would also be terribly low. Most of the array will be empty, as the school will only have a few thousand present and past students.

We can still store the students' records in an array sized to a few thousand. All we need to do is find a way to squeeze our input key range into our array index range. Essentially, this means mapping our nine-digit numeric passport into a four-digit one. This job can be done by what is known as a hash function. A hash function would accept a key (our passport number) and return an array index within the size of our array (see *Figure 3.3*).

We say that a hash function maps our input key universe to our chosen hash range, which in this example is our array size:

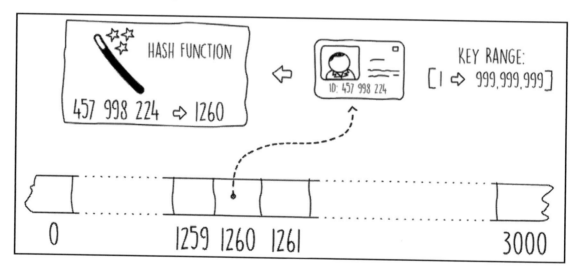

Figure 3.3: Using hash functions

Using a hash function enables us to use a much smaller array and saves us a lot of memory. However, there is a catch. Since we are forcing a bigger key space into a smaller one, there is a risk that multiple keys map to the same hashed array index. This is what is called a **collision**; we have a key hash to an already filled position. The strategy on how to deal with collisions together with the choice of hash function make up our hash table. The following code snippet shows a Java interface that defines our hash table API. We will gradually implement this interface in later sections of this chapter:

```java
public interface HashTable<K,V> {
    void put(K key,V value);
    Optional<V> get(K key);
    void remove(K key);
}
```

Snippet 3.1: Hashtable interface. Source class name: Hashtable

 Go to `https://goo.gl/FK1q6k` to access this code.

In Java, the classes `java.util.Hashtable` and `java.util.HashMap` both implement the interface `HashTable`. The main difference between the two classes is that the `HashMap` is unsynchronized and permits nulls.

In this section, we first introduced direct addressing by looking at an example scenario. Later, we expanded the problem to a bigger key space, showing how hash tables can be used in such a scenario. In the next section, we will see two common solutions for dealing with hash table collisions.

Dealing with Collisions with Chaining

What do we do when two keys hash to the same slot in our array? Overwriting the element in our array is not an option as this would mean losing records. One common solution to deal with collisions is a technique called **chaining**. In this solution, the hash table data is stored outside the actual array itself.

The idea behind chaining is that each entry in our hash array has a pointer to its own linked list. Any items we add to our hash table are stored in these linked lists. Initially, every entry in the array is initialized to contain an empty linked list. Whenever we insert a particular array slot in the hash table, we insert it at the head of the linked list associated with that position. In this way, we can support hash collisions. Another insert, on an already occupied array slot, would result in a new item at the head of its linked list. *Figure 3.4* shows an example in which two entries with different keys have hashed to the same array slot, resulting in the two records stored in the linked list:

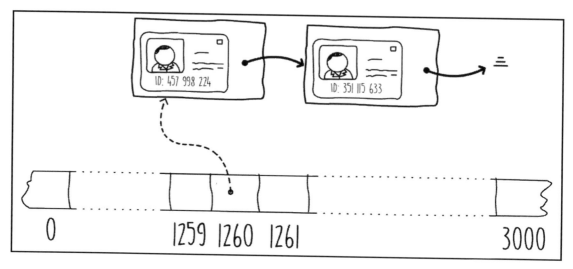

Figure 3.4: Using linked lists to chain multiple entries in one hash slot

Searching for a particular key requires first locating the array slot, and then traversing the linked list, one item at a time, looking for the required key until there is a match or the end of the list is reached. *Snippet 3.2* shows the search (get) and insert (put). The delete (remove) operation can be found by the URL provided after the snippet. We make use of Java's linked list collection for this hash table implementation. In the constructor, the array is initialized with the given capacity, and each element is filled with an empty linked list.

Using the Java linked list collections enables us to use Java's lambda expressions when searching for the key in the `get(key)` method. When searching, we try to match the key with the ones found in the linked list and only return the optional value if a match is found.

Using the lambda expressions also enables us to implement the `delete` operation in a clean manner by just calling the `removeif()` method with a key-matching predicate (the `delete` operation can be found by the URL provided after the code snippet):

```
public void put(K key, V value) {
    int hashValue = hashProvider.hashKey(key, array.length);
    array[hashValue].addFirst(new Pair<>(key, value));
}
public Optional<V> get(K key) {
    int hashValue = hashProvider.hashKey(key, array.length);
    return array[hashValue].stream()
        .filter(keyValue -> keyValue.getKey().equals(key))
        .findFirst()
        .map(Pair::getValue);
}
```

Snippet 3.2: The chained hash table. Source class name: ChainedHashTable

Go to `https://goo.gl/mrzQfY` to access this code.

The best case runtime complexity for the search operation (`get()` method) shown in *Snippet 3.2* when the hash table contains n items is when we have no collisions, resulting in $O(1)$, and the worst is when we have n collisions, resulting in $O(n)$.

The `HashProvider` interface shown in *Snippet 3.2* simply provides us with a method that implements a hash function. We will implement this interface in the following sections when we explore different hash techniques. The runtime complexity for the chained hash table is dictated by how long our linked lists get. The best case is when every single item we insert in the hash table hashes to a different slot, that is, when there are no collisions. In the best case, we have a runtime of $O(1)$ when each linked list only contains one item, and we can directly access any item.

The worst-case is the other extreme, when every single item hashes to the same value, resulting in a linked list with n items. When this happens, the performance degrades to $O(n)$ time to search for the required key. This is because we need to traverse the linked list of n nodes to search the required key.

This worst runtime complexity of $O(n)$ is applicable to all hash tables, not just chained ones. However, on average, and if the right hash function is chosen, the runtime performance of hash tables can be close to $O(1)$.

 A chained hash table has no load limit. Even in situations where none of the slots are empty, we can still add more items to the hash tables by continuing to append to the linked lists. This means that the load factor of a chained hash table can exceed the value of 1.

Chained hash tables are the most popular collision resolution implementation. The reason for this is that they are easy to implement, provide a good performance, and unlike some other techniques, allow the hash table structure to scale dynamically, and grow beyond the load factor of 1. In the next section, we will discuss another solution dealing with collisions, called **open addressing**.

Dealing with Collisions with Open Addressing

In the previous section, we saw how we can deal with collisions using linked lists at each array position. A chained hash table will keep on growing without any load limit. Open addressing is just another way of tackling hash collisions. In open addressing, all items are stored in the array itself, making the structure static with a maximum load factor limit of 1. This means that once the array is full, you can't add any more items. The advantage of using open addressing is that, since you're not using linked lists, you're saving a bit of memory since you don't have to store any pointer references.

You can then use this extra memory to have an even larger array and hold more of your key value pairs. To insert in an open-addressed hash table, we hash the key and simply insert the item in the hash slot, the same as a normal hash table. If the slot is already occupied, we search for another empty slot and insert the item in it. The manner in which we search for another empty slot is called the **probe sequence**.

A simple strategy, shown in *Figure 3.5*, is to search by looking at the next available slot. This is called **linear probing**, where we start from the array index at the hash value and keep on increasing the index by one until we find an empty slot. The same probing technique needs to be used when searching for a key. We start from the hash slot and keep on advancing until we match the key or encounter an empty slot:

Figure 3.5: Linear probing in open addressing

The next code snippet shows the pseudocode for linear probing insert. In this code, after we find the hash value we keep on increasing a pointer by one, searching for an empty slot.

Once we reach the end of the array, we wrap around to the start using the *modulus* operator. This technique is similar to one we used when we implemented array-based stacks. We stop increasing the array pointer either when we find a null value (empty slot) or when we get back to where we started, meaning the hash table is full. Once we exit the loop, we store the key-value pair, but only if the hash table is not full.

The pseudocode is as follows:

```
insert(key, value, array)
  s = length(array)
  hashValue = hash(key, s)
  i = 0
  while (i < s and array[(hashValue + i) mod s] != null)
    i = i + 1
  if (i < s) array[(hashValue + i) mod s] = (key, value)
```

Snippet 3.3: Pseudocode for inserting using linear probing

Searching for a key is similar to the insert operation. We first need to find the hash value from the key and then search the array in a linear fashion until we encounter the key, find a null value, or traverse the length of the array.

If we want to delete items from our open, addressed hash table, we cannot simply remove the entry from our array and mark it as null. If we did this, the search operation would not be able to check all possible array positions for which the key might have been found. This is because the search operation stops as soon as it finds a null.

One solution is to add a flag at each array position to signify that an item has been deleted without setting the entry to null. The search operation can then be modified to continue past entries marked as deleted. The insert operation also needs to be changed so that, if it encounters an entry marked as deleted, it writes the new item at that position.

Linear probing suffers from a problem called **clustering**. This occurs when a long succession of non-empty slots develop, degrading the search and insert performance. One way to improve this is to use a technique called **quadratic probing**. This strategy is similar to linear probing, except that we probe for the next empty slot using a quadratic formula of the form $h + (ai + bi^2)$, where h is the initial hash value, and a and b are constants. *Figure 3.6* shows the difference between using linear and quadratic probing with $a = 0$ and $b = 1$. The diagram shows the order in which both techniques explore the array.

In quadratic probing, we would change *Snippet 3.3* to check at array indexes of the following:

```
array[(hashValue + a*i + b*i^2) mod s]
```

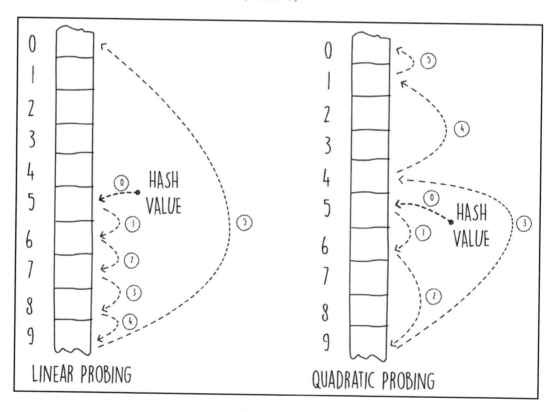

Figure 3.6 Linear versus quadratic probing

Although quadratic probing reduces the effect of clustering, it suffers from a problem called secondary clustering. This is a milder form of clustering, however, it will still degrade performance. In addition, the constants a and b, and the array size need to be carefully chosen so that the probing explores the entire array.

One other probing strategy used in open-addressing hash tables is called **double hashing**. This makes use of another hash function to determine the step offset from the initial hash value. In double hashing, we probe the array using the expression $h + ih'(k)$, where h is the hash value and $h'(k)$ is a secondary hash function applied on the key. The probing mechanism is similar to linear probing, where we start with an i of zero and increase by one on every collision. Doing so results in probing the array every $h'(k)$ step. The advantage of double hashing is that the probing strategy changes on every key insert, reducing the chances of clustering.

In double hashing, care must be taken to ensure that the entire array is explored. This can be achieved using various tricks. For example, we can size our array to an even number and make sure the secondary hash function returns only odd numbers.

Carrying out the Linear Probing Search Operation

The aim here is to develop pseudocode for the search operation in linear probing.

Perform the following steps:

1. Write pseudocode similar to *Snippet 3.3* to show the search operation. The operation should return null if the key is not found in the hash table. The search function should have a signature as follows:

   ```
   search(key, array)
   ```

2. The pseudocode can be developed as follows:

   ```
   search(key, array)
   s = length(array)
   hashValue = hash(key, s)
   i = 0
   while (i < s and array[(hashValue + i) mod s] != null
      and array[(hashValue + i) mod s].key != key)
     i = i + 1
   keyValue = array[(hashValue + i) mod s]
   if (keyValue != null && keyValue.key == key)

      return keyValue.value
   else return null
   ```

Snippet 3.4: Solution pseudocode for searching using linear probing

In this section, we have seen another manner for dealing with hash collisions by keeping all items in the array itself, saving memory, but limiting the structure statically. In the next subsection, we shall go into detail about some of the various hash functions available.

Remainder and Multiplication Hash Functions

For hash tables, a hash function maps a specific key's space into a smaller number range. More formally, a hash function, f, maps keys of a specific data type to integers in a fixed interval $[0,..., N - 1]$. We say $f(x)$ hashes the value of x.

The hash function can accept only numeric data types. To allow us to use hash tables on more complex data types, we usually need to convert all these types into numeric representations. This translation varies, depending on the type of data. For example, a character can be changed into its UTF-8 (or ASCII) numeric equivalent. Converting a full string can be done by converting each character separately and then using a strategy to combine the characters into one value.

In Java, the `hashCode()` method converts an object into a numeric representation, which is ready to be used by a hash function. It is present in the object class and can be overridden using a custom implementation.

There are many techniques on how we can map keys from a wide range into smaller ones. An ideal hash function is one that reduces collisions to a minimum. In other words, when a good hash function is used, each key has the same probability of filling any of the slots in our array. In practice, finding an ideal hash function is very difficult unless we know the input distribution.

A simple technique to implement a hash function is what is known as the **remainder method**. The hash function simply takes in any numeric key, divides it by the table size (size of the array), and uses the resultant remainder as the hash value. This value can then be used as an index on the array.

The following code shows how the remainder hashing method can be implemented in Java using the modulus operator:

```java
public int hashKey(Integer key, int tableSize) {
    return key % tableSize;
}
```

Snippet 3.5: The remainder method. Source class name: RemainderHashing

Go to `https://goo.gl/wNyWWX` to access this code.

The reminder method might result in many collisions if care is not taken when choosing an appropriate table size. Once again, consider the example given in the beginning of this section where we are using the student's passport or national ID number to identify a student in the school. To demonstrate the problem, we use an array-based hash table with a size of 1,000 elements. It just so happens that in the country where the school is based, the last four digits of the passport numbers represent the year of birth of the passport holder.

When using the remainder method in this scenario, all the students with the same year of birth will hash to the same value, causing a lot of collisions on the hash table.

A better choice of a table size is to use a prime number, ideally not too close to the power of 2. For example, the value of 1,447 is a good choice in our example, since it's not too close to 1,024 or 2,048 (2^{10} and 2^{11}) and is also prime. Using this value as a table size for our example would reduce collisions.

Using the remainder method restricts us on the choice of size for our hash table (to reduce the chance of collisions). To address this, we can use a different hashing technique, called the **multiplication method**. In this method, we multiply the key by a constant double value, k, in the range $0 < k < 1$. We then extract the fractional part from the result and multiply it by the size of our hash table.

The hash value is then the floor of this result:

$$hash(x) = \lfloor s(xk \bmod 1) \rfloor$$

Where:

- k is a decimal in the range between 0 and 1
- s is the size of the hash table
- x is the key

Implementing the Multiplication Method for a Hash Table

The aim here is to develop a code in Java for implementing the multiplication method for a hash table.

Perform the following steps:

1. Implement a class with a method which accepts an integer and returns a hash value using the multiplication method shown in this section. The constant k is passed in as the class constructor. The method signature should be:

   ```
   int hashKey(int key, int tableSize)
   ```

2. The following code shows an implementation for the multiplication hash function:

   ```
   private double k;
   public MultiplicationHashing(double k) {
      this.k = k;
   }
   public int hashKey(Integer key, int tableSize) {
      return (int) (tableSize * (k * key % 1));
   }
   ```

   Snippet 3.6: Solution for the multiplication method. Source class name: MultiplicationHashing.

Go to `https://goo.gl/xJ7i1b` to access this code.

In this section, we have seen two basic techniques on how to compute hash values, the remainder method and the multiplication method. Both of these strategies are widely used in hash tables.

In the next section, we will examine yet another mechanism, called **universal hashing**.

Universal Hashing

Both the remainder and multiplication hashing methods have a common vulnerability. If an attacker knows the details of our hash function (table size and any constant values), he/she could devise an input key sequence resulting in a collision on every item, turning our hash table into a linked list and slowing down our program. To address this problem, a hashing technique called universal hashing can be used.

Universal hashing works by choosing a random function from a universal set of hash functions at the start of execution. This makes it difficult for an attacker to guess the exact workings of the hashing technique used. By using this technique, the same sequence of keys will produce a different sequence of hash values on every execution.

A set of hash functions, H, with size n, where each function maps a universe of keys $\cup$ to a fixed range of $[0, s)$, is said to be universal for all pairs, where $a, b \in \cup, a \neq b$ and the probability that $h(a) = h(b)$, $h \in H$ is less than or equal to n/s.

We can construct our set of universal hash functions by using two integer variables, i in a range of $[1, p)$, and j in a range of $[0, p)$, where p is a prime number larger than any possible value of the input key universe. We can then generate any hash function from this set using:

$$h_{ij}(x) = ((ix + j) \bmod p) \bmod s$$

Where s is the size of the hash table and x is the key.

The following code snippet shows a Java implementation of universal hashing suitable for integer-type keys. Note how our implementation makes use of the `BigInteger` class to work out the hash key. This is needed because multiplying a long Java numeric type with a large integer might result in a big enough value that exceeds the maximum capacity of a Java long. The choice of p in this method is such that any integer key input will always have a smaller value, since in Java an integer only has a maximum value of 2^{31}:

```java
public UniversalHashing() {
    j = BigInteger.valueOf((long) (Math.random() * p));
    i = BigInteger.valueOf(1 + (long) (Math.random() * (p - 1L)));
}
public int hashKey(Integer key, int tableSize) {
    return i.multiply(BigInteger.valueOf(key)).add(j)
        .mod(BigInteger.valueOf(p))

        .mod(BigInteger.valueOf(tableSize))
        .intValue();
}
```

Snippet 3.7: Universal hashing for integer keys. Source class name: UniversalHashing

Go to `https://goo.gl/5Kv7qG` to access this code.

Java provides hash tables and built-in hashing mechanisms using the `Object.hashcode()` method. As a result of this, it is very difficult to implement a universal hashing table which integrates with Java's existing `hashcode()` method, since the i and j variables in the preceding code would have to be shared between different objects being inserted in the same table.

For more information and mathematical proofs about why we pick a larger than key prime number, refer to Carter and Wegman, *Universal Classes of Hash Functions, Journal of Computer and System Sciences*: `https://doi.org/10.1016/0022-0000(79)90044-8`.

Universal hashing provides us with good results, minimizing collisions, and is immune to malicious attacks, since the function parameters are chosen at random.

Activity: Implementing Open Addressing

Scenario

We have been asked to develop an algorithm to search and remove data from a hash table using the open addressing technique.

Aim

To implement a hash table using open addressing with linear probing.

Prerequisites

To solve this activity, you have to implement the methods found in the class that is available on GitHub at the following URL:

```
https://github.com/TrainingByPackt/Data-Structures-and-Algorithms-in-Java/blob/
master/src/main/java/com/packt/datastructuresandalg/lesson3/activity/
openaddressing/OpenAddrHashTable.java
```

If you have your project set up, you can run the following unit test for this activity by running:

```
gradlew test --tests
com.packt.datastructuresandalg.lesson3.activity.openaddre
ssing*
```

Steps for Completion

1. Study the pseudocode shown in *Snippet 3.3* and *Snippet 3.4*
2. Implement them in Java
3. Create a container class that will hold your key and value in the hash table
4. Have a flag on this container to indicate when an item is deleted
5. Use this flag in the insert operation to overwrite it if it is deleted

Getting Started with Binary Search Trees

Like hash tables, binary search trees are fast lookup data structures for organizing key value pairs and implement the data dictionary operations. In addition to providing insert, search, and delete, binary tree supports efficient querying such as finding minimum and maximum, successor, and predecessor. When using balanced binary search trees, insert and search operations have a worst-case runtime complexity of *O(log n)*. This is a big theoretical improvement over the worst-case scenario of a hash table, which is *O(n)*.

Binary Tree Structure

The structure of a binary tree is composed of a series of nodes connected together via pointers. *Figure 3.8* shows the fundamental relation between nodes. Each node can have a maximum of two child nodes, a left one and a right one.

Each node (except the top-level node) also has exactly one parent:

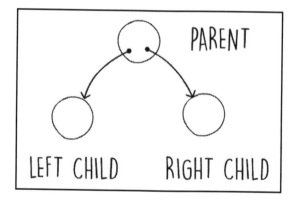

Figure 3.8: Showing a simple binary tree relation

Figure 3.9 shows some more terminology applied to binary trees. In this diagram, we also show that binary tree nodes can hold data items by showing the node storing different shapes. The top-level node is called the root node. The root node in a tree structure is the only node that doesn't have a parent. Nodes that don't have any children are called leaf nodes. The height of a tree is the number of hops it would take you to get from the root node to the furthest leaf node. The diagram shows an example of a tree which has a height of 2.

The height of a tree is an important metric, as it affects the performance. The shallower a tree is (smaller height), the more performant a tree structure is.

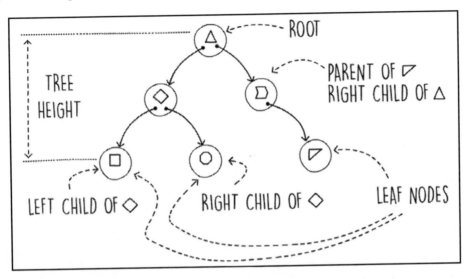

Figure 3.9: Binary tree terminology

Similar to a linked list, the binary tree structure is modeled using pointers and node objects. In a linked list node, we only have a next pointer, referencing the next node in the list. Similarly, in a binary tree node we have two pointers, each one linking to one child. These are the left and right child pointers. The following code snippet shows how we can model the binary tree node using a Java class:

```java
public class BinaryTreeNode<K,V> {
    private BinaryTreeNode<K,V> left;
    private BinaryTreeNode<K,V> right;
    private K key;
    private V value;
    public BinaryTreeNode(K key, V value) {
        this.key = key;
        this.value = value;
    }
}
```

Snippet 3.8: The Binary tree node class. Some getters and setters have been omitted for brevity. Source class name: BinaryTreeNode

Go to `https://goo.gl/D6Jvo2` to access this code.

We can then have another class representing the binary tree itself, where the operations will be implemented. This class only needs to hold a pointer to the root node, since any node can be reached by starting from the root node and navigating down. In the following code snippet, we show an interface declaring the binary tree:

```
public interface BinaryTree<K,V> {
    void put(K key,V value);
    Optional<V> get(K key);
}
```

Snippet 3.9: Binary tree interface. Source class name: BinaryTree.

 Go to `https://goo.gl/jRcLhu` to access this code.

In this section, we have introduced the structure and terminology of binary trees. We then learned how to model each node using Java classes. In the next section, we will continue building on these concepts by introducing binary search trees and implementing the insert and search operations.

Binary Search Tree Operations

Binary search trees are normal binary trees in which data is organized in an ordered manner. Consider the same problem we encountered in the previous section, of the school keeping a student's records by using the passport numbers as a key. *Figure 3.10* shows an example of how you can organize the data in a binary tree.

Note how at each node the left child has a key which is less than its own. On the other hand, the right child has a larger key. Shown in the diagram, the root node has a left child containing a key of a smaller value than the root key. On the other hand, the right child has a key of a larger value than the root.

This rule is repeated through the entire tree. In a binary search tree, the left child will always have a smaller key than the parent, while the right child will have a larger one. Using this binary search tree property, we can create efficient operations on the tree structure:

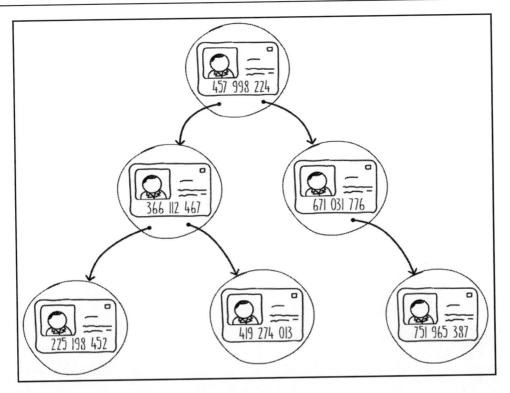

Figure 3.10: An example of a binary search tree

As a result of this simple rule, the tree exhibits important properties. For example, note how all the nodes that are descendants of the left child of the root node have a smaller key than the root. This property is valid for any node of the tree. All keys on the left subtree of a node will always have smaller keys, and vice versa.

Searching in a binary search tree requires us to follow some simple instructions. We start at the root and at each node, we ask ourselves: "*Is the key we're looking for equal to less than, or greater than the key on this node?*" If the key is equal, we're done and we have found our node. If the key is less, we follow the left child pointer, otherwise we follow the right one. We repeat this step until we find our key or hit a *null child pointer*.

Another important property of a binary search tree is being able to easily find the maximum and minimum key in the tree. Finding the maximum key in a binary tree is easy. Conceptually, this is the rightmost node. This can be found by starting at the root and always picking the right child until there isn't any right child to choose. The reverse is valid (picking the left child) for the minimum key.

The following code snippet shows the search implementation. In this implementation, we use the power of recursion to perform the search. We start by checking if the tree is empty by checking whether the root is null. If a root node is present, we compare the key and either return the value or recursively search the child nodes. To compare the key, we assume the provided key implements the comparable interface. Using Java's optional flat mapping makes our implementation much more concise:

```java
public Optional<V> get(K key) {
    return Optional.ofNullable(root).flatMap(n -> get(key, n));
}
private Optional<V> get(K key, BinaryTreeNode<K, V> node) {
    if (((Comparable) key).compareTo(node.getKey()) == 0)
        return Optional.of(node.getValue());
    else if (((Comparable) key).compareTo(node.getKey()) < 0)
        return node.getLeft().flatMap(n -> get(key, n));
    else
        return node.getRight().flatMap(n -> get(key, n));
}
```

Snippet 3.10: Binary search tree search operation. Source class name: SimpleBinaryTree.

Go to `https://goo.gl/xE2GvH` to access this code.

Java's `objectA.compareTo(objectB)` method in the comparable interface returns a negative integer, zero, or a positive integer as `objectA` is less than, equal to, or greater than `objectB`. Thus, the following statement:

```java
((Comparable) key).compareTo(node.getKey()) < 0
```

Is conceptually the same as the following:

```java
key < node.getKey()
```

Inserting in a binary tree follows the same logic as the search operation. We start from the root and keep on looking for a location where we need to create a new node. This is shown in the next code snippet. Like the search operation, this Java implementation is also recursive. If the root node is absent we just create a new one, otherwise we recursively insert the key value pair each time by choosing the left or right child depending on the value of the key.

We have three stopping conditions for the recursive call that are, as follows:

- When the *key is equal* to the one on the node, we simply overwrite the entry
- When the *left child is not present*, we create a new node with the key value pair
- When the *right child is not present*, we create a new node with the key value pair

The following code demonstrates the binary search tree insert operation:

```
if (((Comparable) key).compareTo(node.getKey()) == 0) {
  node.setKey(key);
  node.setValue(value);
} else if (((Comparable) key).compareTo(node.getKey()) <0) {
  if (node.getLeft().isPresent())
    put(key, value, node.getLeft().get());
  else
    node.setLeft(new BinaryTreeNode<>(key, value));
} else {
  if (node.getRight().isPresent())
    put(key, value, node.getRight().get());
  else
    node.setRight(new BinaryTreeNode<>(key, value));
}
```

Snippet 3.11: Binary search tree insert operation. Source class name: SimpleBinaryTree

Go to `https://goo.gl/hHpeiP` to access this code.

Binary tree deletion requires matching the subtree structure with a number of patterns and performing different actions with each case. In some situations, it requires that you connect the subtree with the parent of the deleted node, which can be quite complex. For this reason, the deletion algorithm is beyond the scope of this book. For information on the deletion operation, you may refer to the following sources:

- *The Art of Computer Programming, Volume 3: Sorting and Searching*, by Donald Knuth.
- Paul E. Black, "binary search tree", in Dictionary of *Algorithms and Data Structures* [online], Vreda Pieterse and Paul E. Black, eds. January 26, 2015. Available at `https://www.nist.gov/dads/HTML/binarySearchTree.html`.

Searching for a Minimum Key in a Binary Tree

The aim is to implement a method in Java to search for the minimum key in a binary tree.

Perform the following steps:

1. Add a method to the binary tree implementation with the following signature:

   ```
   public Optional<K> minKey()
   ```

2. The method needs to find the minimum key in the tree and return it. If the tree is empty, it should return an empty optional.

3. Finding the minimum in a binary search tree requires us to always follow the left child node until we reach a node with no left child pointer. The following code demonstrates this:

   ```
   public Optional<K> minKey() {
     return Optional.ofNullable(root).map(this::minKey);
   }
   private K minKey(BinaryTreeNode<K, V> node) {
     return node.getLeft().map(this::minKey).orElse(node.getKey());
   }
   ```

   Snippet 3.12: Minimum key operation. Source class name: SimpleBinaryTree.

Go to `https://goo.gl/YbZz6i` to access this code.

In this section, we have introduced binary search trees and explored how they can be used to organize key value pairs. We also saw how binary search trees can be used for simple range queries, such as finding the maximum and minimum keys. In the next section, we learn about all the different ways we can traverse a binary search tree.

Traversing a Binary Search Tree

Traversing a binary tree is the process of stepping through each node of the tree and performing some sort of action on the data contained in the node (such as printing the key value pair). There are two main techniques to perform tree traversal: depth-first search and breadth-first search, more commonly known as DFS and BFS, respectively.

In depth-first search, the algorithm goes down a path of tree nodes until it cannot go any further. Once it cannot go further, it backtracks and discovers any remaining unexplored branches. A recursive implementation is shown in the following code. In this traversal method, a different output sequence is produced depending on where the action is executed in the method.

In a **preorder** execution, we perform the action immediately, as soon as a new node is discovered. A **postorder** execution, on the other hand, is when both children of a node have been explored and we're about to backtrack. An **inorder** execution is done when the left child has been processed but before processing the right one. When using an inorder traversal, the keys in the binary search trees will be processed in ascending order:

```
public void printDfs() {
    Optional.ofNullable(root).ifPresent(this::printDfs);
}
private void printDfs(BinaryTreeNode<K, V> node) {
    //System.out.println("PREORDER " + node.getKey());
    node.getLeft().ifPresent(this::printDfs);
    System.out.println("INORDER " + node.getKey());
    node.getRight().ifPresent(this::printDfs);
    //System.out.println("POSTORDER " + node.getKey());
}
```

Snippet 3.13: Depth-first search. Source class name: SimpleBinaryTree

Go to `https://goo.gl/xMzkbE` to access this code.

In the breadth-first search traversal, the algorithm explores the binary tree one level at a time, left to right. The traversal starts from the root node and finishes at the leaf nodes. The output of an example binary tree is shown in *Figure 3.11*. To implement a BFS traversal of a binary tree, we can make use of a queue initialized to contain the root node. Then, while the queue is not empty, we read the first node on the queue, process it, and add first the left and then the right child to the queue:

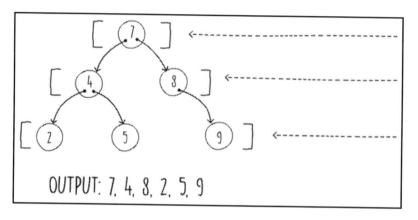

Figure 3.11: Breadth-first search on a binary tree

We show the pseudocode of this as follows:

```
breadthFirstSearch(root)
  if (root != null)
    queue = createQueue()
    enqueue(queue, root)
    while (not isEmpty(queue))
      node = dequeue(queue)
      process(node)
      if (node.left != null) enqueue(queue, node.left)
      if (node.right != null) enqueue(queue, node.right)
```

Snippet 3.14: Pseudocode for breadth-first search

 If we substitute the queue with a stack, the algorithm shown in *Snippet 3.14* changes from breadth-first search to the non-recursive depth-first search. In fact, the way to implement a non-recursive DFS is to make use of a stack.

Activity: Implementing BFS in Java

Scenario

We have been asked to write code to implement an algorithm that searches the binary tree one level at a time, left to right. The traversal starts from the root node and finishes at the leaf nodes.

Aim

To apply BFS traversal in Java.

Steps for Completion

1. Implement the algorithm shown in the preceding code in Java.
2. Use the Java `LinkedList` collection to implement the queue shown in the pseudocode. The method signature should be as follows:

```
public void printBfs()
```

In this section, we have learned about the various ways we can traverse a binary tree and the different ordering produced by each strategy. We have also seen how these algorithms can be implemented both in a recursive and in an iterative manner. In the next section, we will discuss a more restrictive type of binary search tree that ensures our data structure maintains a good performance, even in the worst input case.

Balanced Binary Search Trees

The performance of a binary search tree is proportional to its height. This is because the search and insert operations start from the root and proceed down the tree one node at a time, doing a key comparison at each step. The taller the tree, the more steps are needed to accomplish this. Thus, if we determine the maximum possible height of a binary tree in relation to its input, we can find out the worst runtime complexity.

If we insert keys in a binary tree, by always adding on the right child of the parent node, we end up with a tree similar to the one shown on the left-hand side of *Figure 3.12*. In this diagram, only the right child pointers on each node are being used. We end up with a tree of height *n*, where *n* is the number of items added to our data structure. We get this kind of one-sided tree when the key input pattern is in order.

In the example shown in *Figure 3.12*, we first insert **5** as a root, then **7** is added as the right child, the next is **12** as the next right child, and so on. Always inserting an increasing number results in the next node on the right. This one type of input pattern makes our binary search tree operations (search, insert, and delete) behave in the worst-case runtime of *O(n)*:

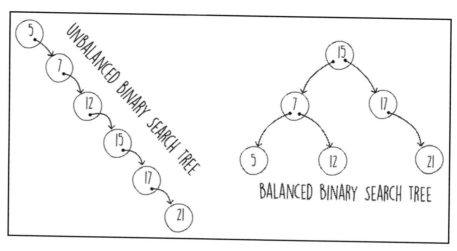

Figure 3.12: Unbalanced versus balanced binary trees

The result is similar if we start from a big number and decrease it each time. We end up with a mirror of the tree shown on the left-hand side of *Figure 3.12*.

The output of a BFS traversal in a normal binary search tree when the key insert order is "1,2,3,4,5,6,7" would be in the same order as the input, that is, "1,2,3,4,5,6,7". We end up creating a new right child at every insert. Since BFS traversal processes one level after another, starting from the root, the traversal output is the same as the input.

In *Figure 3.12*, on the right-hand side, we show another binary tree containing the same keys. This binary tree has been restructured with the effect that the tree is now shorter. Note that the tree is still valid, that is, the left child always has a key that is smaller than its parent, and vice versa. A balanced binary tree has a height of about $log_2 n$.

If we manage to find a way to rebalance the binary search tree at each insert in $O(\log n)$ or better, the worst-case runtime performance for inserts and searches would also be of $O(\log n)$.

Luckily, various algorithms exist that self-balance the tree structure as you perform inserts. Some of the most common ones are as follows:

- AVL trees
- Red black trees
- AA trees

All of these algorithms check that the binary tree is following specific balancing rules at key insert. If, due to a new node being inserted, the tree becomes unbalanced, the self-balancing algorithm kicks in and restructures some of the nodes to keep the tree balanced. The technique to rebalance the nodes relies on tree rotations, where under certain conditions some of the parent and child nodes are rotated. Importantly, these modifications are also performed in the worst-case of $O(\log n)$, meaning that both inserts and searches on binary trees have a worst runtime complexity of $O(\log n)$. In this section, we will examine tree rotations as they are the base operation for most self-balancing trees.

For more information about self-balancing trees, you may refer the following resources:

The Art of Computer Programming, Volume 3: Sorting and Searching by Donald Knuth.

Paul E. Black, "red-black tree", in *Dictionary of Algorithms and Data Structures* [online], Vreda Pieterse and Paul E. Black, eds. 13 April 2015. Available at the link: `https://www.nist.gov/dads/HTML/redblack.html`.

Figure 3.13 shows an example of a left and right rotation. Note how the node being rotated (node **5** in the right rotation and **9** in the left rotation) ends up being the new parent. Importantly, there is a constant number of child pointer reassignments. The properties of a binary search tree are still valid after a tree rotates, that is, a left child pointer always has a smaller key that points to its parent, and vice versa. This means that we can perform any number of these tree rotations and our binary search tree will still be valid:

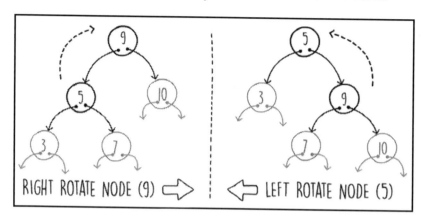

Figure 3.13: Left and right tree rotations

Snippet 3.15 shows how we perform a right rotation in Java. The method accepts a top-level node that needs rotation (node **5** in *Figure 3.13*) and its parent node. The method requires the parent node since it has to reassign its child pointer. Performing the opposite right rotation on the tree node is the mirror image of the following method:

```java
public void leftRotate(BinaryTreeNode<K, V> nodeX,
  BinaryTreeNode<K, V> parent) {
   BinaryTreeNode<K, V> nodeY = nodeX.getRight().get();
   nodeX.setRight(nodeY.getLeft().orElse(null));
   if (parent == null)
     this.root = nodeY;
   else if (parent.getLeft().filter(n -> n == nodeX).isPresent())
     parent.setLeft(nodeY);
   else
     parent.setRight(nodeY);
     nodeY.setLeft(nodeX);
}
```

Snippet 3.15: Java implementation of the left tree rotation. Source class name: SimpleBinaryTree

Go to `https://goo.gl/Ts3JBu` to access this code.

Applying Right Tree Rotation

The aim is to implement a right tree rotation in Java.

Modify *Snippet 3.15* to make the method perform a right tree rotation instead of a left tree rotation. The following code shows the required modification:

```
public void rightRotate(BinaryTreeNode<K, V> nodeX,
  BinaryTreeNode<K, V> parent) {
  BinaryTreeNode<K, V> nodeY = nodeX.getLeft().get();
  nodeX.setLeft(nodeY.getRight().orElse(null));
  if (parent == null)
    this.root = nodeY;
  else if (parent.getRight().filter(n -> n == nodeX).isPresent())
    parent.setRight(nodeY);
  else
    parent.setLeft(nodeY);
    nodeY.setRight(nodeX);
}
```

Snippet 3.16: Java implementation of the right tree rotation. Source class name: SimpleBinaryTree

Go to `https://goo.gl/KKDWUa` to access this code.

The right rotation is an exact mirror image of the left rotation. It's enough to change all the left references with right references and vice versa.

In this section, we saw how we can improve the performance of binary search trees by using tree rotations to balance the data structure. This enables the tree to remain of a shorter height with a runtime complexity of *O(log n)*.

Activity: Retrieving the Successor of an Element When the Tree is Traversed in Inorder

Scenario

We need to write a method that, given a key as an argument, returns the next in order key found in the binary search tree. If the key given as an argument is not found, the method should still return the next in order key. If the binary tree is empty or all the stored keys are smaller than the argument, then the return value should be empty. For example, using a collection of {10, 13, 52, 67, 68, 83} stored in the binary search tree:

- An input of 13 results in 52
- An input of 67 results in 68
- An input of 55 results in 67
- An input of 5 results in 10
- An input of 83 results in `Optional.empty`
- An input of 100 results in `Optional.empty`
- Any input on an empty binary tree results in `Optional.empty`

Both the in order successor and predecessor algorithms have many applications. As an example, think about if you had to keep a scoreboard at some sports event where you only want to show the first three runners. If you keep your data in a binary search tree, you can find the maximum key and then work out the next two predecessor nodes.

 The solution needs to have a runtime complexity of *O(log n)*.

Aim

To retrieve the successor of an element when the tree is traversed in inorder.

Prerequisites

Implement the following method, provided in the `InOrderSuccessorBinaryTree` class that extends the `SimpleBinaryTree` class, which is available on GitHub at the following link:

```
https://github.com/TrainingByPackt/Data-Structures-and-Algorithms-in-Java/blob/
master/src/main/java/com/packt/datastructuresandalg/lesson3/activity/
inordersuccessor/InOrderSuccessorBinaryTree.java
```

```
public Optional<K> inOrderSuccessorKey(K key)
```

If you have your project set up, you can run the unit test for this activity by running:
```
gradlew test --tests
com.packt.datastructuresandalg.lesson3.activity.inordersu
ccessor*
```

Steps for Completion

1. Use a non-recursive search operation first to find the first node with a key equal to or less than the input
2. Realize that the inorder successor can be in only one of two places, either as a parent of this node or the minimum key on the subtree of the right child of this node (if any)

Summary

In this chapter, we have studied two of the most commonly used data structures for implementing the data dictionary operation. Hash tables provide fast in-memory insertion and lookup operations. In addition, binary trees also give us the ability to perform various range queries such as successor, predecessor, minimum and maximum. In this chapter, we have seen examples of both data structures, and implementations of these operations.

4

Algorithm Design Paradigms

In the previous chapter, we learned about hash tables and binary search trees. In this chapter, we will explore algorithm design paradigms. These design patterns can be seen as the generic methods or approaches that motivate the design of a class of algorithms.

Just as an algorithm is a higher abstraction than a computer program, an algorithm design paradigm is an abstraction higher than an algorithm. The choice of an algorithm paradigm is an important one when designing an algorithm.

This chapter will focus on the following three algorithm paradigms:

- Greedy
- Divide and conquer
- Dynamic programming

By becoming familiar with these higher abstractions, you can make more informed decisions when designing algorithms.

 In a previous chapter, we have come across the merge sort and quick sort algorithms, which are examples of the divide and conquer paradigm. As the name suggests, both of these algorithms *divide* the input into smaller parts, which are then solved recursively (*conquer*).

There are obviously more algorithm design paradigms, but these three already cover a broad range of problems. Some other paradigms we're not talking about in this book are backtracking and prune and search. There are even paradigms focused on specific branches of computer science. The sweep line algorithms, in computational geometry, is an example of this.

By the end of this chapter, you will be able to:

- Describe greedy, divide and conquer, and dynamic programming algorithm paradigms
- Analyze common problems solved by using the described paradigms

- List the properties of a problem to be solved by each paradigm
- Solve some well-known problems that explain the applicability of each paradigm

Introducing Greedy Algorithms

Algorithms typically go through a sequence of steps, wherein each step you have a set of choices. Greedy algorithms, as the name suggests, follow the heuristic of making the locally choice at each step, with the hope of arriving at a global optimum. To better understand what we mean by this, let's introduce a problem.

The Activity Selection Problem

Peter is an energetic guy, and usually has many things to do in a given day. However, with the amount of things he wants to do, he is usually unable to do them all in a single day. What he usually does after waking up is write up a list of activities that he has to do, along with their time span. Then, looking at that list, he devises a plan for the day, trying to accommodate as many activities as possible.

Being an energetic guy, he usually rushes through this process and finds himself doing fewer activities than possible throughout the day. Can you help him maximize the amount of activities he can do in a day, given his schedule? An example of a schedule for Peter is given in the following table:

ID	Activity	Time Span
1	Tidy up his room	10:00 - 12:00
2	Going to the rock concert	20:00 - 23:00
3	Play chess at the local club	17:00 - 19:00
4	Take a shower	10:00 - 10:30
5	Dinner with friends	19:00 - 20:30
6	Play Civilization VI	21:30 - 23:00
7	Have lunch with friends	12:30 - 13:30
8	Go to the cinema	20:00 - 22:00
9	Go biking in the park	17:00 - 19:30
10	Go to the beach	16:00 - 19:00
11	Go to the library	15:00 - 17:00

Table 4.1: Peter's schedule

This is known as the **activity selection problem**. The problem is to schedule several competing activities that require exclusive use of a common resource (which is Peter, in this case), with the goal of selecting a maximum size set of activities that are mutually compatible.

In other words, we are trying to find the biggest set of activities that Peter can perform in a day. Each activity (a_i) has a start time (s_i) and a finish time (f_i). Two activities, a_i and a_j, are considered compatible if the intervals (s_i, f_i) and (s_j, f_j) do not overlap, for example, $s_i \geq f_j$ or $s_j \geq f_i$.

Looking at Peter's schedule, and converting the start and finish times to minutes since the start of a day, we can arrive at the following table. To convert the times to minutes since the start of the day, we multiply the hours by 60 and add the minutes. For example, activity 1 runs from 10:00 to 12:00. 10:00 is 600 ($10*60 + 0$) minutes since the start of the day, and 12:00 is 720 ($12*60 + 0$) minutes since the start of the day:

ai	1	2	3	4	5	6	7	8	9	10	11
si	600	1200	1020	600	1140	1290	750	1200	1020	960	900
fi	720	1380	1140	630	1230	1380	810	1320	1170	1140	1020

Table 4.2: Start and finish times of peter's activities

For this example, the subset $\{a_1, a_3, a_5, a_6\}$ consists of mutually compatible activities, as their times don't overlap. It is not a maximum subset (that is, we can find a set with a larger number of activities), since the subset $\{a_3, a_4, a_5, a_6, a_7, a_{11}\}$ is larger (note that the order of the activities is $a_4, a_7, a_{11}, a_3, a_5$ and a_6). In fact, it is a larger subset of mutually compatible activities. It is not the only one: another possible larger subset is $\{a_1, a_7, a_{11}, a_3, a_5, a_6\}$.

How should we approach this problem to find the maximum size set of activities that are mutually compatible? It turns out we should do the greedy choice. What this means is that, at each step of the algorithm, from the set of activities that we can still perform, we should choose one greedily.

The greedy choice may not be immediate, but you can intuitively think that we should select activities that leave Peter available for as many other activities as possible.

We can have two approaches to resolve this problem, and they are as follows:

- Always choose the activity with the earliest starting time; however, we can have the activity with the earliest starting time finishing after all the other activities.
- Choose the activity that consumes the least amount of time; however, we can have a small activity overlapping two or more non-overlapping activities (for example, activities *[1, 4), [3, 5)* and *[4, 8)*).

Hence, both of these approaches don't work.

From the set of activities that we are able to choose, we must choose the first one to finish, as that is the activity that would leave Peter available for as many of the activities that follow it as possible. If we sort activities by finish time, we can then always select the first activity we find that is compatible with the last activity selected for Peter.

Solving the Activity Selection Problem

To implement the greedy algorithm in Java to solve the activity selection problem, as **described previously**.

A possible implementation of the algorithm described to solve the activity selection problem is as follows:

```
Collections.sort(sortedActivities, (o1, o2) -> Integer.signum(o1.finish -
o2.finish));
if (sortedActivities.size() > 0)
  selected.add(sortedActivities.get(0));
for (int i = 1; i < sortedActivities.size(); i++)
  if (sortedActivities.get(i).start >= selected.get(selected.size() -
1).finish)
    selected.add(sortedActivities.get(i));
```

 Navigate to `https://goo.gl/xYT2Ho` to access complete code.

After having sorted the activities by finish time, the selection part of the algorithm runs in *O(n)* time. Since we can't sort in *O(n)*, the overall complexity of this algorithm is bounded by the complexity of the sorting algorithm. As seen in previous chapters, we can sort in *O(nlog(n))* so that's the runtime complexity of the algorithm we've devised for the activity selection problem. The algorithm looks good, but how can we be sure that it always arrives at the optimal solution?

Ingredients of a Greedy Algorithm

There are two basic ingredients every greedy algorithm has in common. They are as follows:

- Optimal substructure property
- Greedy choice property

Optimal Substructure Property

The first step in solving an optimization problem by using a greedy approach is to characterize the structure of an optimal solution. A problem exhibits the optimal substructure property if an optimal solution to the problem within it contains optimal solutions to subproblems.

Intuitively, we can think that the activity selection problem exhibits the optimal substructure property in the sense that, if we suppose that a given activity belongs to a maximum size set of mutually compatible activities, then we are left to choose the maximum size set of mutually compatible activities from the ones that finish before this activity starts and that start after this activity finishes. Those two sets must also be maximum sets for the compatible activities, so that they can showcase the optimal substructure of this problem.

Formally, it is possible to prove that the activity selection problem exhibits optimal substructure. Let's assume we have the set of activities sorted in monotonically increasing order of finish time so that the following can be true for activities i and j:

$$f_i \leq f_j \text{ if } i \leq j$$

Whereas f_i is denoting the finish time of activity i.

Suppose we denote by S_{ij} the set of activities that start after activity a_i finish, and they finish before activity a_j starts. Thus, we wish to find a maximum set of mutually compatible activities in S_{ij}.

Let's say that the set is A_{ij}, and includes activity a_k. By including a_k in an optimal solution, we are left with two subproblems that are finding the maximum subset of mutually compatible activities in the set S_{ik} and set S_{kj}, which can be represented as follows:

$$A_{ij} = A_{ik} \cup \{a_k\} \cup A_{kj}$$

Thus, the size of the maximum size set of mutually compatible activities in S_{ij} is given by the following:

$$|A_{ij}| = |A_{ik}| + |A_{kj}| + 1$$

If we could find a set A'_{kj} of mutually compatible activities in S_{kj} where $|A'_{kj}| > |A_{kj}|$, then we could use A'_{kj} instead of A_{kj} in the optimal solution to the subproblem for S_{ij}. But that way, we would have something that contradicts the assumption that A_{ij} is an optimal solution:

$$|A_{ik}| + |A'_{kj}| + 1 > |A_{ik}| + |A_{kj}| + 1 = |A_{ij}|$$

Greedy Choice Property

When searching for a possible solution to a problem, we usually consider various solutions, which we call the solution space.

When trying to find the best solution to a problem, we're usually interested in a global optimum, that is, the optimal solution from the whole set of possible solutions.

However, the solution space can exhibit other optimums. Namely, we can have local optimums, which are optimal solutions in a small neighborhood of possible solutions.

The greedy choice property states that from a local optimum we can reach a global optimum, without having to reconsider decisions that have already been made.

In the activity selection problem for Peter, we applied the greedy choice by always choosing the activity with the earliest finish time from the set of available activities.

Intuitively, we can think that this problem exhibits the greedy choice property in the sense that if we have a maximum size subset and we replace the activity from that set with the earliest finish time with one that finishes even earlier, we are always left with a maximum size set, making it safe to always choose the one with the earliest finish time.

It is possible to prove that the greedy choice is always part of some optimal solution.

Let's try to prove that, for any nonempty subproblem S_k, if a_m is an activity in S_k with the earliest finish time, then a_m is included in some maximum size subset of mutually compatible activities of S_k.

To prove it, let's assume the following:

- A_k is a maximum size subset of mutually compatible activities in S_k
- a_j is the activity in A_k with the earliest finish time

If $a_j = a_m$, we are done. If $a_j \,!= a_m$, we can try to replace a_j by am in A_k, producing the set $A'_k = A_k - \{a_k\} \cup \{a_m\}$.

We can safely do that since the activities in A_k are disjoined. a_j is the first activity to finish in A_k, and $f_m <= f_j$.

Since $|A'_k| = |A_k|$, we conclude that A'_k is a maximum size subset of mutually compatible activities of S_k, and that it includes a_m.

Intuition usually helps us decide whether a greedy algorithm produces the optimal solution, without having to formally prove the optimal substructure and the greedy choice properties. We're also going to cover a different paradigm of algorithm design in this chapter, which is dynamic programming that also requires problems to exhibit the optimal substructure property. If you are not sure if a greedy algorithm works for a given problem due to the greedy choice, you can always build a dynamic programming solution for it to gain some insight.

Huffman Coding

To gain more insight about greedy algorithms, let's look at another problem that is solvable by a greedy algorithm.

Huffman codes represent a way of compressing data effectively. Data is considered to be a sequence of characters. Huffman's greedy algorithm uses a table with the frequency of each character to build up an optimal way of representing each character as a binary string.

To illustrate this, imagine we have a 1,00,000 character data file that we wish to store in a compressed fashion. The frequency of each character in the data file is given by the following table:

Character	a	b	c	d	e	f
Frequency	45,000	13,000	12,000	16,000	9,000	5,000

Table 4.3: Frequency of each character in a data file

There are various ways to represent this information. For the purpose of this problem, let's say that we want to design a binary character code in which each character is represented by a unique binary string (which we shall call a **code word**). One option is to use a fixed-length code (for example, each character is represented by a code word of the same size). If we opt for that, we need three bits to represent each the six characters, as shown in the following table:

Character	a	b	c	d	e	f
Frequency	45,000	13,000	12,000	16,000	9,000	5,000
Code Word	000	001	010	011	100	101

Table 4.4: Code word for each character

Using this method, we need 3,00,000 bits to code the entire sequence of characters. Can we do better?

A variable-length code can do a lot better than a fixed-length code. Since we want to minimize the size of the compressed sequence of bits, we want to give short code words to frequent characters and long code words to infrequent characters. A possible code for this character sequence is shown in the following table:

Character	a	b	c	d	e	f
Frequency	45,000	13,000	12,000	16,000	9,000	5,000
Code Word	0	101	100	111	1101	1100

Table 4.5: Possible code for character sequence

Instead of 3,00,000 bits, this code requires only 2,24,000 bits to represent the character sequence. Using this code, we save around 28% of space. The code we have presented is also an optimal character code for this sequence, as we shall see.

Building a Huffman Code

Before we start studying an algorithm to solve this problem, we should introduce something called **prefix codes**. Prefix codes are codes in which no code word is also a prefix of some other code word. As you have seen from the proposed variable-length code, we must make sure that no code word is also a prefix of some other code word, since we want to concatenate on code words and unambiguously be able to decode it afterwards.

For example, using the code shown previously, we encode the string `abc` as `0101100`. Since no code word is a prefix of any other, decoding is vastly simplified, as we can identify the initial code word, translate it, and repeat the process on the remainder of the encoded sequence.

A convenient (for decoding purposes) representation of prefix codes is a binary tree whose leaves are the characters of the original data sequence. For the proposed variable-length code, we have the following binary tree:

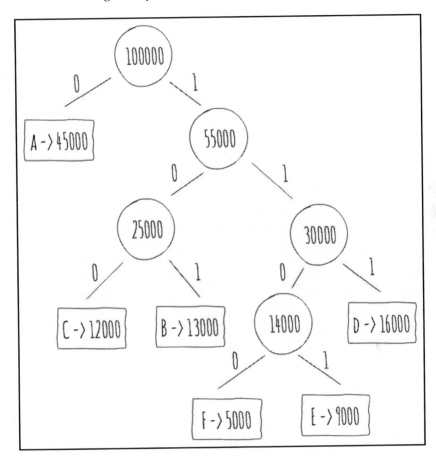

Figure 4.1: A Representation of prefix codes

The binary code word for a character is the path from the root to that character, following in the binary digits in each edge. Note that each node also holds the frequency of characters under its subtree. Such a tree also has some interesting properties. A tree for an optimal prefix code has exactly $|C|$ leaves, C being the alphabet from which the characters are drawn. The number of internal nodes is exactly $|C| - 1$. We also know that the number of bits necessary to encode a particular character in a sequence is equal to the frequency of that character multiplied by the depth of the leaf that holds the character. As such, the number of bits required to encode the full character sequence is simply the sum of these values for all the characters in the alphabet.

If we can build such a tree, we can compute an optimal prefix code. David A. Huffman invented a greedy algorithm to construct an optimal prefix code, called a **Huffman Code**. Its basic idea is to build the tree in a bottom-up fashion. We start with just the leaf, one for each character. We then repeatedly join the two least-frequent nodes, until we are left with a single node, which is the root of the tree.

Developing an Algorithm to Generate Code Words Using Huffman Coding

To implement an algorithm capable of building the tree that generates the binary code words for the character in a data file using Java:

1. Use a priority queue to store nodes with the character frequency.
2. Repeatedly join the two nodes with the least frequencies until you are left with a single node. The source code for this algorithm is as follows:

```java
for (int i = 0; i < N - 1; i++) {
    Node n = new Node();
    n.left = pq.remove();
    n.right = pq.remove();
    n.frequency = n.left.frequency + n.right.frequency;
    pq.add(n);
}
```

Snippet 4.2: Huffman code. Source class name: Huffman

Go to `https://goo.gl/indhgT` to access the full code.

We make use of a priority queue to store our nodes, making it very efficient *(O(logn))* to extract the node with the least frequency. A priority queue is like a queue, or a stack, but each element has an additional **priority** associated with it. An element with a higher priority is served before an element with lower priority. Priority queues are usually implemented using heaps, which usually provide *O(1)* time to find the element with a higher priority, *O(logn)* to insert an element, and *O(logn)* time to remove the element with a higher priority.

To analyze the running time of Huffman's algorithm, let's break it down into steps. We first go through each character in the frequencies map and build a node that we later insert in the priority queue. It takes *O(logn)* time to insert a node in the priority queue. Since we go through each character, it takes *O(nlogn)* to create and initially populate the priority queue. The second for loop executes exactly *n-1* times. Each time, we perform two removes from the priority queue, each one taking *O(logn)* time. In its whole, the `for` loop takes *O(nlogn)* time. We thus have two steps, each taking *O(nlogn)* time, which leaves us at a total running time on a set of *n* characters of *O(nlogn)*.

Activity: Implementing a Greedy Algorithm to Compute Egyptian Fractions

Scenario

For this activity, we will be building a greedy algorithm to compute Egyptian fractions. Every positive fraction can be represented as a sum of unique unit fractions. A fraction is a unit fraction if its numerator is one and its denominator is a positive integer. For example, 1/3 is a unit fraction. Such a representation, for example, a sum of unique unit fractions, is called an Egyptian fraction, since it was used by the ancient Egyptians.

For example, the Egyptian fraction representation of *2/3* is *1/2 + 1/6*. The Egyptian fraction representation of *6/14* is *1/3 + 1/11 + 1/231*.

Aim

To implement a greedy algorithm to compute Egyptian fractions, as described previously.

Prerequisites

- Implement the `build` method of the `EgyptianFractions` class, which returns a list of denominators for the Egyptian fraction representation, in increasing order, which is available on GitHub at:

  https://github.com/TrainingByPackt/Data-Structures-and-Algorithms-in-Java/blob/master/src/main/java/com/packt/datastructuresandalg/lesson4/activity/egyptian/EgyptianFractions.java

- Assume that the denominator is always larger than the numerator, and that the returned denominators always fit in a Long

 To verify that your solution is correct, run `./gradlew test` in the command line.

Steps for Completion

1. Check whether the numerator divides the denominator without leaving a remainder, and that we're left with a single fraction
2. If not, find the greatest possible unit fraction, subtract it from the original fraction, and recur on the remaining fraction

In this first section, we introduced the greedy paradigm of algorithm design using the activity selection problem as a running example. We introduced the two properties a problem must observe to be optimally solved by a greedy algorithm: optimal substructure and greedy choice. To gain intuition about the applicability of greedy algorithms, we later explored two other problems that are solvable by a greedy approach: Huffman coding and Egyptian fractions.

Getting Started with Divide and Conquer Algorithms

In Chapter 2, *Sorting Algorithms and Fundamental Data Structures*, we introduced, among other sorting algorithms, merge and quick sort. A peculiarity of both algorithms is that they divide the problem into subproblems that are smaller instances of the same, solve each one of the subproblems recursively, and then combine the solutions to the subproblems into the solution for the original problem. This strategy forms the basis of the divide and conquer paradigm.

The Divide and Conquer Approach

In a divide and conquer approach, we solve a problem recursively, applying the following three steps at each level of recursion:

- **Divide** the problem into more than one subproblems that are smaller instances of the same problem.
- **Conquer** the subproblems by solving them recursively. Eventually, the subproblem sizes are small enough for them to be solved in a straightforward manner.
- **Combine** the solutions to the subproblems in the solution for the original problem.

When a subproblem is large enough to be solved recursively, we call that the **recursive case**. When a subproblem becomes small enough that recursion is no longer necessary, we say that we have reached to the **base case**. It is common to solve subproblems that are different from the original problem, in addition to the subproblems that are smaller instances of the main problem. Solving these problems is considered to be part of the combine step.

In Chapter 2, *Sorting Algorithms and Fundamental Data Structures*, we saw that the runtime complexity of merge sort was *O(nlogn)*. We can also see that the worst-case running time *T(n)* of merge sort can be described by the following recurrence:

$$T(n) = \begin{cases} O(1) & if \ n = 1, \\ 2T(n/2) + O(n) & if \ n > 1. \end{cases}$$

These kinds of recurrences arise frequently and characterize divide and conquer algorithms. If we generalize the recursion to the following:

$$T(n) = \begin{cases} O(1) & if \ n = 1, \\ aT(n/b) + f(n) & if \ n > 1. \end{cases}$$

Where *a* >= 1, *b* > 1 and *f(n)* is a given function, we have the recurrence for the worst-case running time of a divide and conquer algorithm that creates subproblems, each being of size *1/b* of the original problem, and in which the combine steps together take *f(n)* time.

When it comes to divide and conquer algorithms, it is often easier to come up with this recursion, but harder to derive the runtime complexity. Fortunately, there are at least three methods to provide **O** bounds for these recurrences: the substitution method, the recursion tree method, and the master method. For the purpose of this book, we will only be focused on the master method.

The Master Method

The master method provides a way to solve recurrences of the following form:

$$T(n) = aT(n/b) + f(n)$$

Where:
$a >= 1$ and $b > 1$ are constants, $f(n)$ is an asymptotically positive function

The master method consists of three cases, which will allow you to solve these kind of recurrences quite easily. Before we delve into these three cases, it is important to note that the recurrence is not actually well defined, since n/b may not be an integer. Whether we replace it with the floor or ceiling of the n/b division will not affect the asymptotic behavior of the recurrence.

The big O notation describes the asymptotic upper bound of the growth rate of a function. There are also other notations to describe bounds on the growth rate of functions.

For the purpose of the master method, we're interested in the big-theta notation (Θ) and the big-omega notation (Ω).

The big-theta notation describes the asymptotic tight bound of the growth rate. It's called tight bound because the running time is nailed within a constant factor above and below. It is a tighter bound than $O(n)$.

When we say that an algorithm is $O(f(n))$, we're saying that the running time of the algorithm as n gets larger is at most proportional to $f(n)$.

When we say that an algorithm is $\Theta(f(n))$, we're saying that the running time of the algorithm as n gets larger is proportional to $f(n)$.

The big-omega notation describes an asymptotic lower bound of the growth rate. When we say that an algorithm is $\Omega(f(n))$, we're saying that the running time of the algorithm as n gets larger is at least proportional to $f(n)$.

Having clarified all the necessary notations, we can present the three cases to derive the asymptotic bounds from a recurrence of type $T(n) = aT(n/b) + f(n)$ as follows:

1. If $f(n) = O(n^{\log_b a - \epsilon})$ for some constant $\epsilon > 0$, then $T(n) = \theta(n^{\log_b a}) = O(n^{\log_b a})$
2. If $f(n) = \theta(n^{\log_b a})$, then $T(n) = \theta(n^{\log_b a} \log(n)) = O(n^{\log_b a} \log(n))$
3. If $f(n) = \Omega(n^{\log_b a + \epsilon})$ for some constant $\epsilon > 0$, and if $a\,f(n/b) \leq c\,f(n)$ for some constant $c < 1$ and all sufficiently large n, then $T(n) = T(n) = \theta(f(n)) = O(f(n))$

Note that in all three cases we're comparing the function $f(n)$ with the function $n^{\log_b a}$. This function is usually called the **critical exponent**.

We can see intuitively that the larger of the two functions determines the solution to the recurrence.

In *case 2*, the functions are of the same size, so we multiply by a logarithmic factor.

One other way to see this is that in *case 1*, the work to split and recombine a problem is dwarfed by subproblems; in *case 2*, the work to split and recombine a problem is comparable to subproblems; and in *case 3*, the work to split and recombine a problem dominates the subproblems.

To get some practice on using the master method, let's look at some examples.

For the first case, let's consider the following:

$$T(n) = 9T(n/3) + n$$

For this recurrence, we have $a = 9$, $b = 3$, $f(n) = n$, and thus we have $n^{\log_b a} = n^{\log_3 9} = \theta(n^2)$. Since $f(n) = \Omega(n^{\log_3 3 + \epsilon})$, ϵ being one, we can apply *case 1* of the master theorem and conclude that $T(n) = O(n2)$.

For the second case, let's consider the following:

$$T(n) = 2T(n/2) + 10(n)$$

For this recurrence, we have $a = 2$, $b = 2$, $f(n) = 10n$, and thus we have $n^{\log_b a} = n^{\log_2 2} = O(n)$. Since $f(n) = O(n)$, we can apply *case 2* of the master theorem and conclude that $T(n) = O(n\log n)$.

For the third and final case, let's consider the following:

$$T(n) = 3T(n/4) + n\log(n)$$

For this recurrence, we have $a = 3$, $b = 4$, $f(n) = nlog(n)$, and thus we have $n^{\log_b a} = n^{\log_4 3} = O(n^{0.793})$. Since $f(n) = \Omega(n^{\log_4 3 + \epsilon})$, ϵ being around 0.2, we can apply *case 3* as long as the condition holds for $f(n)$.

For sufficiently large n, we have $af(n/b) = 3(n/4)log(n/4) <= (3/4)nlogn$ *(for c = 3/4)*. Consequently, $T(n) = O(nlogn)$.

The Closest Pair of Points Problem

Now that we know what characterizes a divide and conquer algorithm and are familiar with the master method to derive bounds from recurrences, let's look at a problem solvable by a divide and conquer approach.

The problem we will be looking at is the problem of finding the closest pair of points on a plane. We are given an array of n points in the plane, and we want to find out the closest pair of points in this array. Recall that the distance between two points, p and q, is given by the following:

$$\|pq\| = \sqrt{(p_x - q_x)^2 + (p_y - q_y)^2}$$

Our first approach may be to compute the distance between each pair and return the smallest, for a runtime complexity of $O(n^2)$. The following snippet implements this algorithm:

```java
PointPair bruteForce(List<Point> points) {
    PointPair best = new PointPair(points.get(0), points.get(1));
    for (int i = 2; i < points.size(); i++) {
        for (int j = i - 1; j >= 0; j--) {
            PointPair candidate = new PointPair(points.get(i), points.get(j));
            if (candidate.distance() < best.distance())
                best = candidate;
        }
    }
    return best;
}
```

Snippet 4.3: Brute force for closest pair of points. Source class name: ClosestPairOfPoints

Go to `https://goo.gl/FrRW3i` to access this code.

The proposed algorithm solves this problem, but we can do better by using a divide and conquer approach. The algorithm makes use of a preprocessing step in which it sorts the input array by its *x* coordinate. Then, it proceeds as follows:

1. **Divides** the array into two halves
2. **Recursively** finds the smallest distances in both subarrays (**conquer**)
3. **Combines** the results by taking the minimum distance from both halves and additionally considers pairs so that one point in the pair is from the left subarray and another is from the right subarray

The approach seems straightforward, except for the combine part. After finding the minimum distance *d* from both the left and right subarrays, we have an upper bound of the minimum distance for this subproblem. Therefore, we only need to consider points whose *x* coordinate is closer than *d* to the middle vertical line. We can then sort those points by *y* coordinates and find the smallest distance in the strip, as shown in the following diagram:

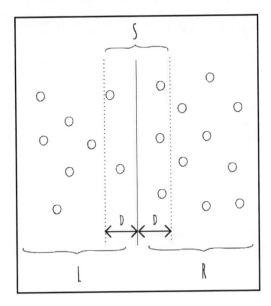

Figure 4.2: Method to calculate closest pair of points

The following code snippet computes the minimum distance in the strip, considering the minimum distance computed so far:

```
Collections.sort(sortedPoints, (o1, o2) -> Integer.signum(o1.y - o2.y));
for (int i = 0; i < points.size(); i++) {
  for (int j = i + 1; j < points.size() &&
      (points.get(j).y - points.get(i).y) < best.distance(); j++) {
    PointPair candidate = new PointPair(points.get(i), points.get(j));
    if (candidate.distance() < best.distance())
      best = candidate;
  }
}
```

Snippet 4.4: Computing the minimum distance between pairs of points in the middle strip. Source class name: ClosestPairOfPoints

Go to `https://goo.gl/PwUrTc` to access the full code.

Looking at this code, it seems to have a runtime of $O(n^2)$, which doesn't really improve our brute force approach. However, it can be proved geometrically that for every point in the strip, a maximum of seven points after it need to be checked. This reduces the runtime of this step to $O(nlogn)$ due to the sorting step.

You can refer to `http://people.csail.mit.edu/indyk/6.838-old/handouts/lec17.pdf` for the geometric proof of the preceding problem.

We can even do better on this step if we sort the initial input by the y coordinate and keep a relationship between the points on the x-sorted array and the y-sorted array, effectively reducing the runtime of this step to $O(n)$.

After having computed the minimum distance from both subarrays and the middle strip, we have found the closest pair of points in the subarray. The following code snippet exposes the merging part of both subarrays and calling the `bestWithStrip()` method:

```
PointPair bestSoFar = bl;
if (br.distance() < bl.distance())
   bestSoFar = br;
List<Point> strip = new ArrayList<>();
for (int i = 0; i < N; i++) {
   if (Math.abs(points.get(i).x - midPoint.x) < bestSoFar.distance())
       strip.add(points.get(i));
}
return bestWithStrip(strip, bestSoFar);
```

Snippet 4.5: Combine Step of the divide and conquer algorithm to find the closest pair of points on a plane. Source class name: ClosestPairOfPoints

 Go to `https://goo.gl/wyQkBc` to access this code.

The proposed algorithm divides all points into two sets and recursively solves both subproblems. After dividing, it finds the strip in $O(n)$ time and finds the closest points in $O(n)$ time (we're assuming the improvement of not requiring the sort in this step). Therefore, $T(n)$ can be expressed as $T(n) = 2T(n/2) + O(n) + O(n) = 2T(n/2) + O(n)$, which is a bound of $O(n\log n)$, being better than the brute force approach.

Activity: Solving the Maximum Subarray Problem

Scenario

Create an algorithm to solve the maximum subarray problem. Find the non-empty, contiguous subarray of the input array whose values have the largest sum. You can see an example array with the maximum subarray indicated in the following diagram:

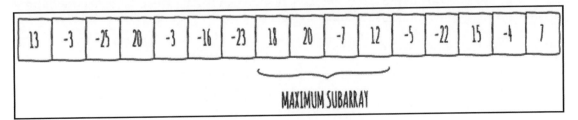

The $O(n^2)$ brute force algorithm that tests all combinations for the start and end indices of the subarray is trivial to implement. Try to solve this using the divide and conquer algorithm.

Aim

To design and implement an algorithm to solve the maximum subarray problem with a better runtime than the $O(n^2)$ brute force algorithm, using a divide and conquer approach.

Prerequisites

- You need to implement the `maxSubarray()` method of the `MaximumSubarray` class in the source code, which returns the sum of values for the maximum subarray of the input array. The code is available on the following path: `https://github.com/TrainingByPackt/Data-Structures-and-Algorithms-in-Java/blob/master/src/main/java/com/packt/datastructuresandalg/lesson4/activity/maxsubarray/MaximumSubarray.java`

- Assume that the sum always fits in an int, and that the size of the input array is at most 100,000.

 The source code comes with a test suite for this class, so to verify that your solution is correct, run `./gradlew test` in the command line.

Steps for Completion

The divide and conquer approach suggests that we divide the subarray into two subarrays of as equal size as possible. After doing so, we know that a maximum subarray must lie in exactly one of following three places:

- Entirely in the left subarray
- Entirely in the right subarray
- Crossing the midpoint

The maximum subarray of the arrays on the left and right is given recursively, since those subproblems are smaller instances of the original problem.

Find a maximum subarray that crosses the midpoint.

There exists an even faster dynamic programming algorithm with a runtime of $O(n)$ to solve the maximum subarray problem. The algorithm is called Kadane's algorithm. Dynamic programming will be explored in the next section.

In the second section, we introduced the divide and conquer paradigm of algorithm design. We formalized the steps that a divide and conquer algorithm goes through, and showed the students how to go from a recurrence relationship to a runtime complexity bound using the master theorem. To gain intuition about the applicability of divide and conquer algorithms, we explored the problem of finding the closest pair of points on a plane.

Understanding Dynamic Programming

After greedy and divide and conquer, we will turn our attention to dynamic programming. Dynamic programming is an algorithm design paradigm that also attempts to solve optimization problems by combining solutions with subproblems. Unlike divide and conquer, subproblems need to exhibit optimal substructure for dynamic programming to be applicable.

Elements of a Dynamic Programming Problem

There are two key ingredients that an optimization problem must have for dynamic programming to be applicable: optimal substructure and overlapping subproblems.

Optimal Substructure

Optimal substructure is something we already covered when we introduced greedy algorithms. Recall that a problem exhibits optimal substructure, if an optimal solution to the problem contains within it, the optimal solutions to the sub-problems. There's a common pattern when trying to discover optimal substructure for a problem that can be explained as follows:

- Show that a solution to the problem consists of making a choice, which leaves one or more subproblems to be solved. This choice may not be obvious and it is likely that many choices have to be tried (contrary to a greedy approach, in which a single optimal choice is made).
- Supposing that you are given the choice that leads to an optimal solution, determine the subproblems that follow.

- Show that the solutions to the subproblems used within an optimal solution to the problem must themselves be optimal
- Usually, a *cut-and-paste* technique is used here. By supposing that each subproblem solution is not optimal, if a non-optimal solution is *cut out* and an optimal one is *pasted in*, a better solution to the original problem is produced, contradicting the supposition that the original solution to the problem was optimal

Overlapping Subproblems

Another ingredient that optimization problems must have for dynamic programming to apply is that the space of subproblems should be **small**. Hence, a recursive algorithm for the problem should solve the same subproblems repeatedly. Typically, the total number of distinct subproblems is a polynomial in the input size. A recursive algorithm is said to have overlapping subproblems if it visits the same problem repeatedly. It's therefore typical for dynamic programming algorithms to cache solutions to subproblems to avoid re-computation of the same solutions over and over.

0-1 Knapsack

To showcase a dynamic programming solution, exploring the properties of the problem that make it solvable by this technique, we shall look at the **0-1 knapsack** problem.

You are given weights and values of n items. You must put these items in a knapsack of capacity W to get the maximum value of the knapsack. You cannot break an item. You can either pick it or not pick it (hence the *0-1* property).

In other words, you are given two arrays, *values[0...n-1]* and *weights[0...n-1]*, which represent values and weights associated with n items, respectively. You want to find the maximum value subset of *values[]* such that the sum of weights of the subset is smaller than or equal to W.

The first immediate solution to this problem is to consider all subsets of items and calculate the total weight and value of all subsets, considering only those whose total weight is smaller than W. To consider all subsets of items, we can observe that there are two choices for each item: either it is included in the optimal subset, or it is not. Hence, the maximum value we can obtain from n items is the maximum of two values:

1. The maximum value obtained by *n-1* items and W weight (that is, they don't include the nth item in the optimal solution)

2. The value of the nth item plus the maximum value obtained by *n-1* items and *W* minus the weight of the nth item (for example, including the nth item)

With the previous observation, we've shown the optimal substructure property for the *0-1* knapsack problem.

Solving the 0-1 Knapsack Problem Using Recursion

To write a code for solving the *0-1* knapsack problem by implementing the recursive approach.

Remember that this is a recursive top-down approach, thus it repeatedly computes the same subproblems for an exponential runtime complexity (2^n). The following code snippet solves this problem using a recursive approach:

```
public int recursiveAux(int W, int weights[], int values[], int n) {
   if (n == 0 || W == 0)
      return 0;
   if (weights[n - 1] > W)
      return recursiveAux(W, weights, values, n - 1);
   return Math.max(values[n - 1] +
      recursiveAux(W - weights[n - 1], weights, values, n - 1),
      recursiveAux(W, weights, values, n - 1));
}
```

Snippet 4.6: Recursive solution for the 0-1 Knapsack problem. Source class name: Knapsack

Go to `https://goo.gl/RoNb5L` to access this code.

The following diagram of tree shows the recursion for *n* and *W*, with inputs *values[] = {10, 20, 30}* and *weights[] = {1, 1, 1}*:

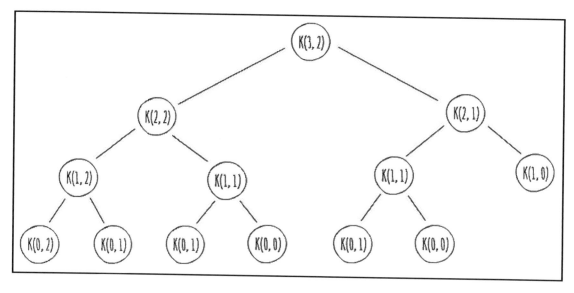

Figure 4.3: Tree Showing the recursion for N and W

Since problems are evaluated again, this has the overlapping subproblems property. When we have a recursive top-down approach to a problem with the overlapping subproblems property, we can improve things by modifying the procedure to save the result of each subproblem (in an array or hash table). The procedure now first checks to see whether it has previously solved the subproblem. If so, it returns the saved value; if not, it computes, stores, and returns it. It is said that the recursive procedure has been memoized, remembering what results it has computed previously. Such an approach is therefore usually called top-down with memoization. The following code snippet adapts the previous one to use memoization:

```
public int topDownWithMemoizationAux(int W, int weights[], int values[],
int n, int[][] memo) {
  if (n == 0 || W == 0)
    return 0;
  if (memo[n][W] == -1) {
    if (weights[n - 1] > W)
      memo[n][W] = topDownWithMemoizationAux(W, weights, values,
              n - 1, memo);
    else
      memo[n][W] = Math.max(
        values[n - 1] + topDownWithMemoizationAux(W - weights[n - 1],
        weights, values, n - 1, memo),
```

```
        topDownWithMemoizationAux(W, weights, values, n - 1, memo));
    }
    return memo[n][W];
}
```

Snippet 4.7: Top down with memoization approach for the 0-1 knapsack problem. Source class name: Knapsack

 Go to `https://goo.gl/VDEZ1B` to access this code.

By applying memoization, we reduce the runtime complexity of the algorithm from exponential (2^n) to quadratic ($n*W$). It is also possible to solve this problem using a bottom-up approach.

Use of a bottom-up approach typically depends on some natural notion of the *size* of the subproblems. We must sort the subproblems by size and solve them in order, smallest first, so that we're sure that we already have computed the solutions for smaller subproblems when we need them for a larger one.

A bottom-up approach usually yields the same asymptotic running time as a top-down approach, but it is typical for it to have much better constant factors, since it has less overhead for procedure calls. A bottom-up approach for solving the *0-1 Knapsack* problem is shown in the following code snippet:

```
public int topDownWithMemoizationAux(int W, int weights[],
    int values[], int n, int[][] memo) {
    if (n == 0 || W == 0)
        return 0;
    if (memo[n][W] == -1) {
        if (weights[n - 1] > W)
            memo[n][W] = topDownWithMemoizationAux(W, weights,
                values, n - 1, memo);
        else
            memo[n][W] = Math.max(
                values[n - 1] +
                topDownWithMemoizationAux(W - weights[n - 1],
                weights, values, n - 1, memo),
                topDownWithMemoizationAux(W, weights,
                values, n - 1, memo));
    }
    return memo[n][W];
}
```

Go to `https://goo.gl/bYyTs8` to access this code.

Longest Common Subsequence

Now, let's look at a different problem which is solvable by a dynamic programming algorithm. The problem we're now interested in is the longest common subsequence problem.

 The difference between a subsequence and a substring is that a substring is a consecutive subsequence. For example, [a, d, f] is a subsequence of [a, b, c, d, e, f], but not a substring. [b, c, d] is a substring and a subsequence of [a, b, c, d, e, f].

We're interested in finding similarities between two given sequences by computing the **Longest Common Subsequence (LCS)** between them. A common subsequence, S_3, of two given sequences, S_1 and S_2, is a sequence whose elements appear in both S and S_2 in the same order, but not necessarily consecutively. This problem is usually applicable when finding DNA similarities of different organisms.

For example, if we have two strands, S_1 and S_2, as follows:

$S_1 = ACCGGTCGAGTGCGCGGAGCCGGCCGAA$
$S_2 = GTCGTTCGGAATGCCGTTGCTCTGTAAAA$

Then the longest common strand between those two, let's call it S_3, would be as follows:

$S_3 = GTCGTCGGAAGCCGGCCGAA$

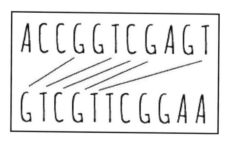

Figure 4.4: Calculating the longest common subsequence

This problem is solvable using dynamic programming. If we go for a brute force approach, we can enumerate all subsequences of S_1 and check each subsequence to see if it is also a subsequence of S_2, keeping track of the longest one we find.

However, if $|S_1| = m$, then S_1 has $2m$ subsequences, making it impractical for long sequences. The **LCS** exhibits the optimal-substructure property.

One way for this to become evident is to think in terms of prefixes. Let's assume that we have the following two sequences:

$X = \{x_1, x_2... x_m\}$
$Y = \{y_1, y_2... y_n\}$

Let Z be any LCS of X and Y that can be represented as follows:

$Z = \{z_1, z_2... z_k\}$

Then, the following cases are possible:

1. If $x_m = y_n$, then $z_k = x_m = y_n$, and therefore Z_k-1 is a LCS of X_m-1 and Y_n-1
2. If $x_m \mathrel{!=} y_n$, then $z_k \mathrel{!=} x_m$ implies that Z is a LCS of X_m-1 and Y
3. If $x_m \mathrel{!=} y_n$, then $z_k \mathrel{!=} y_n$ implies that Z is a LCS of X and Yn-1

This tells us that an LCS of two sequences contains the LCS of prefixes of the two sequences, exhibiting the optimal-substructure property. If we define $c[i][j]$ to be the length of a LCS of sequences X_i and Y_j, then we can arrive at the following recursive formula, which guides us toward the dynamic programming solution for the problem that can be represented as follows:

$$c[i][j] = \begin{cases} 0 & if \ i = 0 \ or \ j = 0, \\ c[i-1][j-1] + 1 & if \ i,j > 0 \ and \ x_i = y_i, \\ max(c[i][j-1], c[i-1][j]) & if \ i,j > 0 \ and \ x_i \neq y_i. \end{cases}$$

Looking at the recurrence, the property of overlapping subproblems immediately pops out.

To find a LCS of X and Y, we may need to find the LCS's of X and Y_{n-1} and X_{m-1} and Y, but each of these have the problem of finding the LCS of X_{m-1} and Y_{n-1}. Many other subproblems share sub-subproblems.

Using this recurrence, in a bottom-up fashion (where we have solutions for subproblems readily computed), we can produce the following dynamic programming algorithm to compute the length of the longest common subsequence of two strings:

```java
public int length(String x, String y) {
    int m = x.length();
    int n = y.length();
    int[][] c = new int[m + 1][n + 1];
    for (int i = 1; i <= m; i++) {
        for (int j = 1; j <= n; j++) {
            if (x.charAt(i - 1) == y.charAt(j - 1))
                c[i][j] = c[i - 1][j - 1] + 1;
            else
                c[i][j] = Math.max(c[i - 1][j], c[i][j - 1]);
        }
    }
    return c[m][n];
}
```

Snippet 4.9: Computing the length of the longest common subsequence of two Strings using dynamic programming algorithm. Source class name: LongestCommonSubsequence

 Go to `https://goo.gl/4TdNVQ` to access this code.

It is possible to also compute the longest common subsequence, and not only the length of it if we keep track of the **direction** we go in the c matrix on each step (either up or left), taking into account that we only add a new character to the optimal subsequence when $x_i = y_j$.

We don't cover the solution to this problem in this book. If you are interested in it, the Wikipedia page for the LCS problem has a detailed walkthrough on the implementation of it: `https://en.wikipedia.org/wiki/Longest_common_subsequence_problem`.

Activity: The Coin Change Problem

Scenario

In this activity, we will be building a dynamic programming algorithm to solve the coin change problem. Given a value, N, if we want to split it into coins, and we have an infinite supply of each of $S=\{S_1, S_2, ..., S_m\}$ valued coins, in how many ways can we do it? The order of the coins doesn't matter. For $N = 4$ and $S = \{1, 2, 3\}$, there are four solutions: $\{1, 1, 1, 1\}$, $\{1, 1, 2\}$, $\{2, 2\}$, and $\{1, 3\}$, so the result should be four.

Aim

To solve the coin change problem as described previously using a dynamic programming algorithm.

Prerequisites

You need to implement the `ways()` method of the `CoinChange` class, which returns the number of ways to produce a given change for amount N, given a set of coins. It is available on the following path:

```
https://github.com/TrainingByPackt/Data-Structures-and-Algorithms-in-Java/blob/
master/src/main/java/com/packt/datastructuresandalg/lesson4/activity/
coinchange/CoinChange.java.
```

 The source code comes with a test suite for this class, so to verify that your solution is correct, run `./gradlew test` in the command line.

Steps for Completion

1. When going through a coin S_m, in order to count the number of solutions, we can divide the solution into two sets:
   - Those that do not contain any coin S_m
   - Those that contain at least one S_m

2. If *w[i][j]* counts the number of ways to make change for *i* using coins up to S_j, then we have the following recursion:

$$
W[i][j] \begin{cases}
1 & if \ i = 0, \\
W[i][j-1] & if \ i - S_i < 0, \\
W[j][j-1] \ + \ W[i - S_j][j] & if \ i - S_j \geq 0.
\end{cases}
$$

In this third and final section, we introduced the dynamic programming paradigm of algorithm design, using the *0-1* knapsack and the longest common subsequence problems as examples. We introduced the two properties a problem must observe to be optimally solved by a dynamic programming algorithm: optimal substructure and overlapping subproblems, and showed the students how to identify these properties. We've also seen the differences between a top-down (with memoization) and a bottom-up approach in dynamic programming algorithms.

Summary

In this chapter, we have discussed three different algorithm design paradigms. We've seen example problems for all of them and discussed how we can identify whether problems may be solvable by one of the given paradigms. In the next chapter, we will be focusing on some string matching algorithms that use the paradigms introduced here.

5
String Matching Algorithms

String matching algorithms are quite common in text-editing programs. These kind of programs frequently need to find all occurrences of a pattern in the text, where the text is usually the document being edited and the pattern is a word supplied by the user. Since text-editing programs aim to be responsive, having efficient algorithms to solve the string matching problem is fundamental.

By the end of this chapter, you will be able to:

- List common string matching algorithms
- Solve the string matching problem
- Devise a naive algorithm to solve the string matching problem
- Implement the Boyer-Moore string search algorithm to carry out string search in literature

Naive Search Algorithm

The string matching problem has two inputs, as follows:

- An array $T[1, 2, ...n]$ of length n
- An *array P[1, 2, ...m]* of length m (<= n)

The elements of T and P are characters from the same finite alphabet (usually called Σ).

For instance, we may be searching in binary strings, in which case our alphabet is {0, 1}, or we may be searching in strings of lowercase letters, in which case our alphabet is {a, b... z}.

The following diagram represents this terminology:

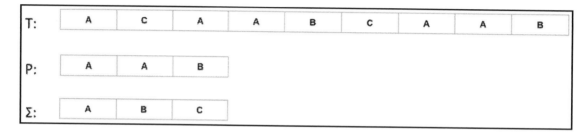

Figure 5.1: Representation of text array T, pattern array P, and finite alphabet Σ

The character arrays P and T are usually called "strings of characters". We're interested in finding occurrences of pattern P in text T.

We say that pattern P occurs in text T if we can align the pattern P with text T so that all characters in P match the ones in T. When aligning, we need to shift pattern P zero or more times to the right.

Therefore, in the string matching problem, we're interested in valid shifts with which pattern P occurs in text T. We say that the pattern P occurs with a shift s in text T if the pattern P occurs beginning at position s + 1 in text T. In other words, we need to shift P from the start of text T s times to the right, in order to find a match. In its essence, the string matching problem aims to find all valid shifts with which pattern P occurs in a given text T.

Two common examples, besides text-editing programs, are finding patterns in DNA sequences and finding web pages that are relevant to queries in internet search engines.

Now that we've formalized the string matching problem, let's look at the naive algorithm to solve it.

Implementing Naive Search

As we described the string matching problem, we said that we were interested in finding all valid shifts with which pattern P occurs in a given text T. If we translate that notion directly into an algorithm, we're able to arrive at the naive string matching algorithm.

Developing the String Matching Algorithm in Java

The aim is to write a code in Java to apply a naive string matching algorithm.

We need to build the naive string matching algorithm. For this algorithm, we need to return all valid starting positions (or shifts) in the text T in which the pattern P occurs.

Perform the following steps:

1. Implement the `match()` method of the `NaiveStringMatching` class, which available on GitHub at the following path:
   `https://github.com/TrainingByPackt/Data-Structures-and-Algorithms-in-Java/blob/master/src/main/java/com/packt/datastructuresandalg/lesson5/activity/naivestringmatching/NaiveStringMatching.java`

2. Repeatedly shift pattern P along text T, matching all the characters in it with the characters aligned in T.

3. When a match occurs, keep track of the index in T where it did.

The implementation of the naive string matching algorithm is an almost direct translation of the problem statement. We want to go through all possible shifts for P and check which ones are valid by comparing each element of P with the corresponding shifted elements of T.

A possible solution for this problem is in the following snippet:

```
for (int i = 0; i < n - m + 1; i++) {
  boolean hasMatch = true;
  for (int j = 0; j < m; j++) {
    if (P.charAt(j) != T.charAt(i + j)) {
      hasMatch = false;
      break;
    }
  }
  if (hasMatch)
    shifts.add(i);
}
```

Snippet 5.1: Solution to the naive string matching problem. Source class name: solution.NaiveStringMatching

Go to `https://goo.gl/PmEFws` to access this code.

Rationalization of the Naive Search Algorithm

The naive search algorithm takes $O((n - m + 1)m)$ time, which is a tight bound on the worst case. We can imagine a worst case of the naive search algorithm if we have a text string with the character a repeating for n times, that is, an (such as $a5 = $ "$aaaaa$"), and the pattern am (for $m <= n$). In this case, we have to execute the inner loop m times to validate the shift.

The naive search algorithm can be improved if we know that all characters in pattern P are different. In this case, whenever we fail validating a shift because $P[j]$ doesn't match $T[i + j]$, we don't need to backtrack. Instead, we can start validating the next shift on $(i + j)$, therefore reducing the running time of the algorithm to $O(n)$.

For example, if $P = $ "$abcd$" and $T = $ "$abcaabcd$", when $i = 0$ and $j = 3$, we find a mismatch ('a' $!= $ 'd'). Instead of repeating the comparisons for $i = 1$, we can start on $i = 3$, because we're sure there's no other a between $i = 0$ and $i = 3$ (remember that all characters of P are different). These kinds of observations on the pattern P are the basis of the Boyer-Moore algorithm.

In this first section, we introduced the string matching problem and solved it using a naive algorithm. In the following section, we'll introduce a much more efficient algorithm to solve this problem—the Boyer-Moore algorithm.

Getting Started with the Boyer-Moore String Searching Algorithm

The Boyer-Moore string searching algorithm was introduced by Robert S. Boyer and J. Strother Moore in 1977, and builds upon the naive search algorithm by intelligently skipping certain sections of the text.

One key feature of the algorithm is that it matches the pattern from right to left, instead of left to right, using to its advantage a couple of shift rules that improve its running time. To understand the effect of these rules, let's build the Boyer-Moore algorithm from our naive search algorithm.

We'll start by modifying the matching on the pattern so that it operates from right to left. The following code demonstrates this:

```
for (int j = m - 1; j >= 0; j--) {
    if (P.charAt(j) != T.charAt(i + j)) {
        hasMatch = false;
        break;
    }
}
```

Snippet 5.2: Modifying the inner loop from Snippet 5.1 for algorithm to operate from right to left C

Using the naive string matching algorithm as the base, let's look at some rules that allow us to intelligently skip certain shifts.

The Bad Character Rule

The idea of the bad character rule is to identify mismatches between a character in the pattern and a character in the text so that we can safely skip certain shifts. To identify the occurrence of a bad character, let's look at the example in the following table:

i	0	1	2	3	4	5	6	7	8	9	10	11	12	13	14	15	16
T	H	C	B	B	A	H	C	C	A	B	A	H	A	H	B	C	C
P	A	B	A	H	A	H											

Table 5.1: Identifying bad characters

In the example provided in *Table 5.1*, we successfully matched the suffix *AH*, but then arrived at a bad character, since $B != H$. Whenever this happens, we're sure that it will only be possible to find a valid shift starting from the next shift that solves this mismatch. This means that we can shift P until either of the following conditions are true:

- The mismatch is turned into a match
- The pattern moves past the mismatched character

We can turn a mismatch into a match whenever the pattern has characters to the left of the mismatched character that match the character in the text. Otherwise, we must move the pattern past the mismatched character. In the example provided in *Table 5.1*, we have another *B* at *P[1]*, so we can shift *P* until *P[1]* aligns with *T[3]* as follows:

i	0	1	2	3	4	5	6	7	8	9	10	11	12	13	14	15	16
T	H	C	B	B	A	H	C	C	A	B	A	H	A	H	B	C	C
P			A	B	A	H	A	H									

Table 5.1.1: Using the bad character rule to skip a shift

We've safely skipped the check for *1* shift. Now, we have a mismatch right in the first character. Let's try to apply the bad character rule. First, let's see if we can turn the mismatch into a match.

Unfortunately, that is not possible because the character *C* is absent from *P*. In this case, we shift the pattern past the mismatched character as follows:

i	0	1	2	3	4	5	6	7	8	9	10	11	12	13	14	15	16
T	H	C	B	B	A	H	C	C	A	B	A	H	A	H	B	C	C
P									A	B	A	H	A	H			

Table 5.1.2: Pattern moving past a mismatched character

We've successfully skipped checking five shifts and have arrived at a valid shift.

The bad character rule will help us optimize the naive string matching algorithm, but only if we can efficiently find the correct number of times to shift. Let's assume we have access to a two-dimensional array *[1...m][1...e]*, *e* being the size of our alphabet. For convenience, let's call this array left and assume that *left[i][j]* gives us the closest index *k* of character *j* in *P* so that *k < i*, or is *-1* if character *j* isn't found to the left of *i* in *P*. If we're able to build such an array, we could improve our naive string search algorithm by considering possibly larger skips (given by the information in left). The following code snippet shows how we can use the left array to improve our naive string searching algorithm as follows:

```
int skip;
for (int i = 0; i < n - m + 1; i += skip) {
  skip = 0;
  for (int j = m - 1; j >= 0; j--) {
    if (P.charAt(j) != T.charAt(i + j)) {
      skip = Math.max(1, j - left[j][T.charAt(i + j)]);
      break;
    }
  }
  if (skip == 0) {
```

```
        shifts.add(i);
        skip = 1;
    }
}
```

 Go to `https://goo.gl/cCYnfp` to access this code.

We're left to filling in the `left` array, which will be performed in the next activity.

Activity: Implementing the Bad Character Rule

Scenario

We have to preprocess string *P* to build the `left` array that allows us to use the bad character rule efficiently. Recall that *left[i][j]* should return either of the following:

- The largest index *k* so that $k <= i$ and $P[k] = j$
- *-1*, if *j* isn't found in *P*

Aim

To build an array that allows us to use the bad character rule efficiently.

Steps for Completion

1. Implement the commented part of the `match()` method of the class `BadCharacterRule`, which is available on GitHub at the following path: `https://github.com/TrainingByPackt/Data-Structures-and-Algorithms-in-Java/blob/master/src/main/java/com/packt/datastructuresandalg/lesson5/activity/badcharacterrule/BadCharacterRule.java`
2. Assume that the alphabet of strings *P* and *T* consists only of lowercase letters of the English alphabet.

The Good Suffix Rule

The good suffix rule presents a complementary method to enhance our search for valid shifts. To identify when the good suffix rule is applicable, let's look at the example given in the following table:

i	0	1	2	3	4	5	6	7	8	9	10	11	12	13	14	15	16	17
T	A	A	B	A	B	A	B	A	C	B	A	C	A	B	B	C	A	B
P	A	A	C	C	A	C	C	A	C									

Table 5.2: Illustration of the good suffix rule

When found in a situation where we have matched a suffix of *P* but have found a mismatch, using the good suffix rule, and considering *t* as the matched suffix, we can try to find the next shift that solves the mismatch by carrying out either of the following cases:

- Find another occurrence of *t* to the left in *P*
- Find a prefix of *P* which matches a suffix of *t*
- Move *P* past *t*

Considering case 1, we can try to shift *P* by three to align other occurrences of *t* in *P* (starting at *P[4]*). As we can see, the letter to the left of that occurrence of *t* (in *P[3]*) is *C*, which is exactly the same as the one that provoked the mismatch. Therefore, we should always try to find a *t* that is followed, on the left, by a character that is different from the one that provoked the mismatch. A variant of the good suffix rule which ignores the character on the left of *t* is called the weak good suffix rule.

 The good suffix rule takes into account that the character on the left of *t* is also called the strong good suffix rule.

If we can't find another occurrence of *t* in *P*, the best we can do with this rule is to find a prefix of *P* that matches a suffix of *t*, entering case 2. *Table 5.3* illustrates this case:

i	0	1	2	3	4	5	6	7	8	9	10
T	A	A	B	A	B	A	B	A	C	B	A
P	A	B	B	A	B						

Table 5.3: Finding prefix of P matching the suffix of T

In this case, we found a mismatch at *P[1]*, but we can't find another occurrence of *BAB* to the left of it. We can, however, find a prefix of *AB* that matches a suffix of *t AB* and shift *P* so that these align.

Whenever we can neither find another occurrence nor a prefix of *t*, we're left with moving *P* past *t* in *T*.

The implementation of the good suffix rule also requires some preprocessing on *P*. To understand the preprocessing that is necessary, we need to introduce the concept of a border and proper prefix and suffix. A prefix of string *S* is a substring of *S* that occurs at the beginning of *S*. A proper prefix of string *S* is a prefix of *S* that is different than *S* (consider that *S* is always a prefix of *S*).

A suffix of string *S* is a substring of *S* that occurs at the end of *S*. A proper suffix of string *S* is a suffix of *S* that is different from *S* (consider that *S* is always a suffix of *S*). A border is a substring of a given string that is both a proper prefix and a proper suffix. For example, given the string *ccacc*, there are two borders: *c* and *cc*. *cca* is not a border.

The preprocessing step for the good suffix rule is divided into two steps: one for case 1 of the rule, and another for case 2.

In case 1, the matching suffix is a border of a suffix of a pattern. For example, if *P* = *AACCACCAC* and we have *t* = *AC* (a suffix of *P*), then we need to find a suffix of *P* that has *AC* as a prefix (constituting a border of the suffix). The string *ACCAC* is a suffix of *P* and has *AC* as a border.

Therefore, we need to find the borders of the suffixes of the pattern. But, even after finding them, we need to be able to map a given border to the shortest suffix that has this border so that we're able to shift accordingly. Moreover, to follow the strong good suffix rule, the border cannot be extended to the left by the same symbol that caused the mismatch.

The preprocessing algorithm for case 1 is displayed in the following snippet:

```java
int i = m, j = m + 1;
int[] f = new int[m + 1];
int[] s = new int[m + 1];
f[i] = j;
while (i > 0) {
    while (j <= m && P.charAt(i - 1) != P.charAt(j - 1)) {
        if (s[j] == 0)
            s[j] = j - i;
        j = f[j];
    }
    i--; j--;
    f[i] = j;
}
```

Snippet 5.4: Preprocessing algorithm for Case 1 of the good suffix rule. Source class name: GoodSuffixRule

Go to `https://goo.gl/WzGuVG` to access this code.
To better understand the preprocessing algorithm for case 1, put
some `println` statements on the relevant steps of the algorithm and run
it using some sample input. You can use string ABBABAB, whose output is
shown in *Table 5.4*.

In the previous snippet, we compute an array *f*, whose entries *f[i]* contain the starting
position of the widest border of the suffix of the pattern that starts at position *i*. *f[m]* is equal
to *m + 1*, as the empty string has no border. The idea behind the previously shown
preprocessing algorithm is to compute each border by checking whether a shorter border
that is already known can be extended to the left by the same symbol. The array *s* is used to
store shift distances; we can save entries in array *s* whenever we can't extend a border to the
left (when *P[i - 1] != P[j - 1]*), provided that *s[j]* is not already occupied.

To better understand what this algorithm produces, let's look at its output for string
ABBABAB, which is shown in the following table:

i	0	1	2	3	4	5	6	7
P	A	B	B	A	B	A	B	
f	5	6	4	5	6	7	7	8
s	0	0	0	0	2	0	4	1

Table 5.4: Output of the preprocessing algorithm for Case 1 of the good suffix rule with string ABBABAB

The widest border of suffix *BABAB*, which starts at 2, is *BAB*, which starts at 4, and
therefore *f[2] = 4*. The widest border of suffix *AB*, which starts at 5, is "", which starts at 7.
Therefore, *f[5] = 7*. The suffix *BABAB*, whose widest border is *BAB*, cannot be extended to
the left (since *P[1] != P[3]*). Therefore, the shift distance of *BAB* is matched and then a
mismatch occurs, which is *s[4] = 4 - 2 = 2*. The suffix *BABAB* has border *B* as well, which
also cannot be extended to left, which ensures that *s[6] = 6 - 2 = 4*. The suffix *B* beginning at
position 6 has border "", beginning at position 7; therefore, *s[7] = 7 - 6 = 1*, which
corresponds to the shift distance if nothing has matched.

In case 2, a suffix of the matching suffix of the pattern occurs at the beginning of the pattern, which constitutes a border of the pattern. Therefore, the pattern can be shifted as far as its widest border allows. What we need to do for the preprocessing step for case 2 is to find, for each suffix, the widest border of the pattern that is contained in that suffix. We can build upon the *f* array that was previously computed to do that. The following snippet illustrates this:

```
j = f[0];
for (i = 0; i <= m; i++) {
  if (s[i] == 0)
  s[i] = j;
  if (i == j)
  j = f[j];
}
```

Snippet 5.5: Preprocessing algorithm for Case 2 of the good suffix rule. Source class name: GoodSuffixRule

Go to `https://goo.gl/ckoTu6` to access this code.

The widest border of the pattern is stored at *f[0]*. The idea of the preprocessing algorithm for case 2 is to use that value until the pattern becomes shorter than *f[0]*, in which case we go with the next wider border of the pattern (*f[j]*).

Integrating the good suffix case with the naive search algorithm allows us to improve on the skips performed, as shown in the following code:

```
for (i = 0; i < n - m + 1; i += skip) {
  boolean hasMatch = true;
  skip = 0;
  for (j = m - 1; j >= 0; j--) {
    if (P.charAt(j) != T.charAt (i + j)) {
      skip = s[j + 1];
      hasMatch = false;
      break;
    }
  }
  if (hasMatch) {
    shifts.add(i);
    skip = s[0];
  }
}
```

Snippet 5.6: The Boyer-Moore algorithm using only the good suffix rule. Source class name: Goodsuffixrule

Go to `https://goo.gl/1uCgeh` to access this code.

Application of the Boyer-Moore Algorithm

The Boyer-Moore algorithm is typically used with one or both the bad character and good suffix rule. When used with both rules, the shift that is to occur is the biggest one produced by the rules. The Boyer-Moore algorithm improves the naive search algorithm in the average case, but is still *O(nm)* in the worst case (that case being the same described in the previous section, that is, a repeated group of characters both in the pattern and in the text).

Implementing the Boyer-Moore Algorithm

The aim is to write a code in Java to implement the Boyer-Moore algorithm.

We need to integrate the bad character rule with the good suffix rule to produce the complete Boyer-Moore algorithm. The idea here is to use the rule that gives us the better (or biggest) shift in each situation.

Perform the following steps:

1. Implement the `match()` method of the `BoyerMoore` class, which is available on the following path:
   `https://github.com/TrainingByPackt/Data-Structures-and-Algorithms-in-Java/blob/master/src/main/java/com/packt/datastructuresandalg/lesson5/activity/boyermoore/BoyerMoore.java`
2. Combine the snippets and change the skip logic to choose the best of both rules.

The following snippet shows how the combined matching can be implemented as a solution:

```
for (i = 0; i < n - m + 1; i += skip) {
  skip = 0;
  boolean hasMatch = true;
  for (j = m - 1; j >= 0; j--) {
    if (P.charAt(j) != T.charAt(i + j)) {
      hasMatch = false;
      skip = Math.max(s[j + 1], j - left[j]
      [T.charAt(i + j)]);
      break;
    }
```

```
    }
  if (hasMatch) {
    shifts.add(i);
    skip = s[0];
  }
}
```

Snippet 5.7: Implementation of the boyer-moore algorithm. Source class: BoyerMoore

 Go to `https://goo.gl/71mXd6` to access this code.

In this section, we've introduced the Boyer-Moore algorithm as an improvement over the naive search algorithm. By preprocessing the pattern to skip unnecessary shifts, we can decrease the average runtime complexity of the string matching algorithm. In the following section, we will list some other string matching algorithms, listing their applicability, but without going into much detail about their implementation.

Introducing Other String Matching Algorithms

Even though the Boyer-Moore string search algorithm is the standard benchmark for practical string search literature, there are other string matching algorithms that are also suitable for different purposes. In this small section, we present the following three, which are the most famous ones:

- Rabin-Karp
- Knuth-Morris-Pratt
- Aho-Corasick

However, only give out the implementation of Rabin-Karp.

Rabin-Karp

In 1987, Richard M. Karp and Michael O. Rabin proposed a string matching algorithm that performs well in practice and generalizes string matching against a set of patterns. The Rabin-Karp algorithm takes $O(m)$ time in its preprocessing stage and its worst-case running time is $O((n - m + 1)m)$, similar to Boyer-Moore's.

To better introduce the Rabin-Karp algorithm, let's assume that our alphabet Σ is composed only of decimal digits (Σ = {0, 1, 2, 3, 4, 5, 6, 7, 8, 9}), so that we can view a string of k characters as a decimal number with length k. Therefore, string 12345 corresponds to number 12345. Given a pattern $P[0...m]$ and a substring from text $T[i...i + m]$, if we convert both those strings to their correspondent decimal number, so that we have numbers p and t_i, then $p = t_i$ only if $P[0...m] = T[i...i + m]$, and therefore i is only a valid shift if $p = t_i$.

If we could compute p in $O(m)$ time and all the t_i values in $O(n - m + 1)$ time, then we could determine all valid shifts in $O(n)$ time by comparing p with each of the t_i values. The problem with this is when p and t_i are too large to work with. If the numbers are too large, then we can work with them modulo q, for a suitable modulus q.

Let's leave the choice of a suitable modulus q for later. How we can generalize this to work with other alphabets? For example, what if we want to use characters that are not decimal digits?

Consider that, in the case of our original alphabet, to convert a string 12345 into a number, we would perform the operation $10^4*1+10^3*2+10^2*3+10^1*4+10^0*5$. If we have a D-ary alphabet {0, 1... d - 1}, then we could use the same strategy, but replace 10 by d. One other consideration to have is that, when we have computed t_i and we want to compute t_{i+1}, then we can simply remove the leftmost digit, shift everything to the left, and add the newest digit, that is, $t_{i+1} = ((t_i - T[i]*d_{m-1})*d + T[i + 1]) \% q$.

One final consideration to have is that working with modulo q is not perfect. $t_i = p \ (mod \ q)$ does not imply that $t_i = p$. But if $t_i \mathrel{!=} p \ (mod \ q)$, then $t_i \mathrel{!=} p$. We can therefore use this as a fast heuristic test to rule out invalid shifts.

Applying the Rabin-Karp Algorithm

The aim here is to develop a code in Java for implementing the Rabin-Karp algorithm for matching a string from a set of alphabetical characters that have decimal digits.

Perform the following steps:

1. Convert the text and pattern strings into digits.
2. Use if and for loops to calculate the number of matching characters.
3. Put everything together to implement the Rabin-Karp algorithm. The following *Snippet 5.9* shows the pre-compute part of the algorithm:

```
long q = BigInteger.probablePrime(31, new  Random()).longValue();
// Precompute d^(m-1) % q for use when removing leading digit
long dm = 1;
```

```
for (int i = 1; i <= m - 1; i++)
   dm = (d * dm) % q;
// Precompute p and t0
long ph = 0;
long th = 0;
for (int i = 0; i < m; i++) {
   ph = (d * ph + P.charAt(i)) % q;
   th = (d * th + T.charAt(i)) % q;
}
```

Snippet 5.9: Implementation of the Rabin-Karp algorithm. Source class name: RabinKarp

Go to `https://goo.gl/w7yzPA` to access this code.

In the previous implementation, we chose q as a large prime number (using the `BigInteger` API). We did that so that we have a good hash function and avoided the most of false positives from the $p = t_i$ comparison. This is a similar technique to the one we saw in the remainder method for hash tables in `Chapter 3`, *Hash Tables and Binary Search Trees*.

Despite being outside the scope of this book, the Rabin-Karp algorithm generalizes well to having a set of patterns to be found in the same text. For that purpose, it is frequently used in plagiarism detection.

Knuth–Morris–Pratt

The **Knuth-Morris-Pratt (KMP)** algorithm is a single-pattern string searching algorithm conceived by Donald Knuth and Vaughan Pratt in 1970, and independently by James H. Morris, being jointly published by the three in 1977. When compared to the Boyer-Moore algorithm, KMP employs the observation that, when a mismatch occurs, the pattern embodies sufficient information to determine where the next match could begin.

It is similar to Boyer-Moore in the sense that it efficiently skips unnecessary comparisons. The KMP algorithm has a running time of $O(n)$.

Aho–Corasick

The Aho-Corasick algorithm is a string searching algorithm invented by Alfred V. Aho and Margaret J. Corasick. Similar to the extended version of the Rabin-Karp algorithm, it is capable of matching elements of a dictionary (set of words) within an input text. The idea behind it is to build a finite state machine that enables matching all strings of the dictionary simultaneously. The algorithm is linear in the length of the strings, plus the length of the searched text, plus the number of output matches. If n is the length of the searched text, m is the sum of the length of all words in the dictionary, and z is the total number of occurrences of words in the text.

Therefore, the time complexity of the Aho-Corasick algorithm is $O(n + m + z)$. In this small section, we've looked at three other famous string matching algorithms. Without going into much detail about them, we've seen their applicability on different problems other than the one the Boyer-Moore algorithm solves. In particular, we've noted that there are algorithms specialized for the finding of a set of patterns in a text.

 In 1979, Zvi Galil introduced an important optimization, called the Galil rule, that speeds up the comparisons done at each shift by skipping sections that are known to match. Using the Galil rule, the Boyer-Moore algorithm achieves linear time complexity in the worst case.

Summary

In this chapter, we have introduced the string matching problem. We've started from the naive search algorithm and improved it by using the rules introduced by Boyer and Moore. We've seen how these rules improve the average runtime complexity of our algorithm. We've also explored some other string matching algorithms without going into too much detail about them. In the next chapter, we will be exploring graphs and their applications

6

Graphs, Prime Numbers, and Complexity Classes

Graph problems are very common in computer science, and their applications pervade many real-life applications. Everything that can be represented by entities and their relationships can ultimately be modeled by a graph. How we connect with friends on social media, how route-planning applications are able to find the shortest route, and how e-commerce websites are able to provide us with recommendations are all examples of problems modeled by graphs.

A graph is a structure composed of a set of objects in which some pairs of objects are related. The objects are modeled by the mathematical abstraction of vertices (sometimes also called nodes), and the pairwise relationships are modeled by the mathematical abstraction of edges (sometimes also called arcs).

Edges can be directed or undirected. A directed edge is an edge which has a direction associated with it. A graph that is composed of directed edges is called a directed graph. A graph that is composed of undirected edges is called an undirected graph. In a directed edge, it is common to call the start of the edge the head and the end of the edge the tail. In a directed graph, the out-degree of a vertex is the number of edges whose head is adjacent to it. The in-degree of a vertex is the number of edges whose tail is adjacent to it.

Figure 6.1 gives an example of a directed graph with six nodes and eight edges, as follows:

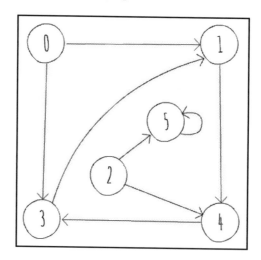

Figure 6.1: A directed graph

Figure 6.2 gives an example of an undirected graph with five nodes and seven edges, as follows:

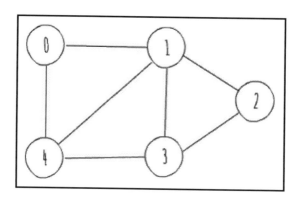

Figure 6.2: An undirected graph

Before we dive into how to represent a graph in a computer program, it is important to describe how the runtime of graph algorithms is usually characterized. As previously stated, a graph, G, can be seen as a set of vertices and edges, that is, $G = (V, E)$. As such, the size of the input is usually measured in terms of the number of vertices ($|V|$) and the number of edges ($|E|$). So, instead of relying solely on a single input size, N, the runtime of graph algorithms usually refers to both $|V|$ and $|E|$. In big O notation, it is common to use V to denote $|V|$ and E to denote $|E|$. For example, an algorithm that runs in time proportional to the number of vertices multiplied by the number of edges is said to run in time $O(VE)$.

Representing Graphs

There are usually two standard ways to represent a graph $G = (V, E)$ in a computer program:

- As a collection of adjacency lists
- As an adjacency matrix

You can use either way to represent both directed and undirected graphs. We'll start by looking at the adjacency list representation.

Adjacency List Representation

The adjacency list representation of a graph consists of an array of $|V|$ lists, one for each vertex in V. For each vertex u in V, there's a list containing all vertices v so that there is an edge connecting u and v in E. *Figure 6.3* shows the adjacency list representation of the directed graph in *Figure 6.1*:

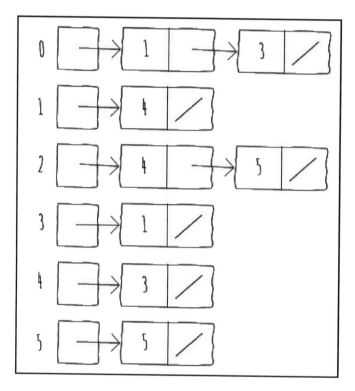

Figure 6.3: Adjacency list representation of the directed graph in Figure 6.1

For undirected graphs, we follow a similar strategy and build the adjacency list as if it were a directed graph with two edges between each pair of vertices u and v, which are *(u, v)* and *(v, u)*.

Figure 6.4 shows the adjacency list representation of the undirected graph in *Figure 6.2*:

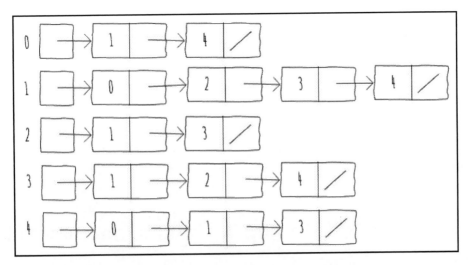

Figure 6.4: Adjacency list representation of the undirected graph in Figure 6.2

If G is a directed graph, the sum of the lengths of all the adjacency lists is $|E|$, as each edge constitutes a single node in one of the adjacency lists.

If G is an undirected graph, the sum of the lengths of all the adjacency lists is $2*|E|$, since each edge (u, v) appears twice, that is, once in u's and once in v's adjacency list.

For both types of graphs, the adjacency list representation has the property of requiring an amount of memory equal to $O(V + E)$.

The following code snippet shows how to create a graph using the adjacency list representation in Java:

```java
public class AdjacencyListGraph {
    ArrayList<Integer>[] adj;
    public AdjacencyListGraph(int nodes) {
        this.adj = new ArrayList[nodes];
        for (int i = 0; i < nodes; i++)
            this.adj[i] = new ArrayList<>();
    }
    public void addEdge(int u, int v) {
        adj[u].add(v);
    }
}
```

Snippet 6.1: Implementation of an adjacency list representation of a graph. Source class name: Adjacencylistgraph

Go to `https://goo.gl/Jrb2jH` to access this code.

It is common for one to have weighted graphs, that is, graphs in which each edge has an associated weight. The adjacency list representation is robust enough to support different graph variants, since we can store different edge representations in the adjacency lists.

We can store different edge representations in adjacency lists because we store the edges themselves, thereby allowing customizable representations.

Writing a Java Code to Add Weights to the Directed Graph

The aim is to adapt the implementation of the `AdjacencyListGraph` class to support weights on edges.

The steps should be the following:

1. Understand *Snippet 6.1* showing how we can implement the adjacency list representation

2. Adapt the implementation so that the array list can store the weights

```java
ArrayList<Edge>[] adj;
public AdjacencyListWeightedGraph(int nodes) {
    this.adj = new ArrayList[nodes];
    for (int i = 0; i < nodes; i++)
    this.adj[i] = new ArrayList<>();
}
public void addEdge(int u, int v, int weight) {
    this.adj[u].add(new Edge(u, v, weight));
}
```

Snippet 6.2: Implementation of an adjacency list representation of a weighted graph. Source class name: Adjacencylistweightedgraph

Go to `https://goo.gl/uoazxy` to access this code.

Adjacency Matrix Representation

The adjacency list representation of a graph provides a compact way to represent sparse graphs, for example, those for which $|E|$ is much less than $|V|^2$. Even though it is a representation that is useful for a lot of algorithms (which we will visit later), it does not support some features. For example, one cannot quickly tell whether there is an edge connecting two given vertices. In order to determine if u and v are connected, one has to go through the adjacency list of u to find an edge connecting it to v. Since the adjacency list of u can have at most E edges, this procedure runs in $O(E)$ time. One alternative representation that remedies this disadvantage at the cost of using asymptotically more memory is the adjacency matrix representation.

The main disadvantage of adjacency list representation of a weighted graph representation is that we can't quickly determine if a given edge (u, v) is present in the graph.

In this representation, a graph $G = (V, E)$ is represented by a $|V|$ x $|V|$ matrix $A = (a_{ij})$, where a_{ij} equals 1 if there's an edge (i, j) and 0 otherwise. The following table shows the adjacency matrix representation of the directed graph of *Figure 6.1*:

	0	1	2	3	4	5
0	0	1	0	1	0	0
1	0	0	0	0	1	0
2	0	0	0	0	1	1
3	0	1	0	0	0	0
4	0	0	0	1	0	0
5	0	0	0	0	0	1

Table 6.1: Adjacency matrix representation of the directed graph of Figure 6.1

The following table shows the adjacency matrix representation of the undirected graph of *Figure 6.2*:

	0	1	2	3	4
0	0	1	0	0	1
1	1	0	1	1	1
2	0	1	0	1	0
3	0	1	1	0	1
4	1	1	0	1	0

Table 6.2: Adjacency matrix representation of the undirected graph of Figure 6.2

The adjacency matrix representation of a graph requires $O(V^2)$ memory, independent of the number of edges in the graph. One thing to note on the adjacency matrix representation of undirected graphs is that the matrix is symmetrical along the main diagonal, since *(u, v)* and *(v, u)* represent the same edge. As such, the adjacency matrix of an undirected graph is its own transpose $(A = A^T)$. Taking advantage of this symmetry, one can cut on the memory needed to store the graph almost in half, as you don't need the array of each vertex to have size *V*. If *i* tracks the index of vertices in *V*, the size of *array[i]* can decrease by one as *i* increases by one.

The following code shows how to create a graph using the adjacency matrix representation in Java:

```java
public class AdjacencyMatrixGraph {
    int[][] adj;
    public AdjacencyMatrixGraph(int nodes) {
        this.adj = new int[nodes][nodes];
    }
    public void addEdge(int u, int v) {
        this.adj[u][v] = 1;
    }
}
```

Snippet 6.3: Implementation of an adjacency matrix representation of a directed graph. Source class name: AdjacencyMatrixGraph

 Go to `https://goo.gl/EGyZJj` to access this code.

The adjacency matrix representation is also robust enough to support different graph variants. In order to support weighted graphs, for example, one can store the weight of the edge in a_{ij}, instead of just one. The adjacency list representation is asymptotically at least as space-efficient as the adjacency matrix representation, but adjacency matrices are simpler, so they might be preferable when the graphs are reasonably small or dense. As previously stated, a sparse graph is one in which $|E|$ is much less than $|V|^2$, whereas a dense graph is one in which $|E|$ is closer to $|V|^2$. The adjacency list representation is more memory-efficient for sparse graphs. For dense graphs, an adjacency matrix representation is better suited, as it possibly takes less memory due to list pointers.

Activity: Building the Adjacency Matrix Representation of a Weighted Undirected Graph

Scenario

Creating an adjacency matrix for a weighted undirected graph to be used for social networking website.

Aim

To write a code in Java for implementing the adjacency matrix representation of a weighted undirected graph.

Prerequisites

For this activity, you have to implement methods `addEdge()` and `edgeWeight()` of class `AdjacencyMatrixWeightedUndirected` available at the following URL:

```
https://github.com/TrainingByPackt/Data-Structures-and-Algorithms-in-Java/blob/
master/src/main/java/com/packt/datastructuresandalg/lesson6/activity/weightedun
directed/AdjacencyMatrixWeightedUndirected.java
```

The methods should add an edge and return the edge weight between two vertices, respectively.

Steps for Completion

1. Start storing the weights of edges in each cell of the matrix. Since we're dealing with undirected graphs, both *(u, v)* and *(v, u)* refer to the same edge, so we need to update both accordingly.

2. It is also possible to not repeat the weight assignment. We just have to be careful and always choose one of *(u, v)* or *(v, u)* when referring to that edge. One possible strategy is to always use *(min(u, v), max(u, v))*. Using that strategy, we also don't need to store the full matrix, thereby saving some space.

In this first section, we learned two different ways of representing a graph in a computer program. We briefly examined the pros and cons of each representation, and we will take a look at their usefulness when implementing graph algorithms in the following sections.

Traversing a Graph

A common activity on a graph is visiting each vertex of it in a given order. We will start by introducing the breadth-first search, and then follow with depth-first search. Both of these techniques form the archetype for many important graph algorithms, as we will see later with the cycle detection and Dijkstra's algorithm for single-source shortest paths.

Breadth-First Search

Given a graph $G = (V, E)$ and a source vertex s, breadth-first search explores the edges of G systematically to discover every vertex that is reachable from s. While doing so, it computes the smallest number of edges from s to each reachable vertex, making it suitable to solve the single-source shortest path problem on unweighted graphs, or graphs whose edges all have the same weight.

Breadth-First Search (BFS) is named so because it expands the frontier between discovered and undiscovered vertices uniformly across the breadth of the frontier. In that sense, the algorithm first explores vertices at distance k from s before discovering vertices at distance $k + 1$. To keep track of progress, breadth-first search identifies each vertex as undiscovered, discovered, or expanded. All vertices start out undiscovered. A vertex is discovered the first time it is encountered during search, and is expanded when all the vertices adjacent to it have been discovered.

BFS constructs a breadth-first tree, rooted at source vertex s. Whenever the search discovers an undiscovered vertex v when scanning the outward edges of already discovered vertex u, the vertex v and the edge *(u, v)* are added to the tree. Therefore, u becomes the parent of v in the breadth-first tree. Since a vertex is discovered at most once, it has at most one parent.

In order to illustrate this, let's look at a run of breadth-first searches for the directed graph of *Figure 6.1*, starting at node 2, in the following table:

Step	Current Node	Discovered	Expanded	Undiscovered	Tree
0	2	{2}	{}	{0, 1, 3, 4, 5}	
1	4	{2, 4, 5}	{2}	{0, 1, 3}	
2	5	{2, 4, 5, 3}	{2, 4}	{0, 1}	
3	3	{2, 4, 5, 3, 1}	{2, 4, 5}	{0}	
4	1	{2, 4, 5, 3, 1}	{2, 4, 5, 3}	{0}	
5	-	{2, 4, 5, 3, 1}	{2, 4, 5, 3, 1}	{0}	

Table 6.3: A Run of BFS on the directed graph of Figure 6.1, starting at node 2

There are a lot of insights to take from the breadth-first tree. For instance, the path from the root to a given node in the tree is the shortest path (in terms of edges) from those two vertices. Another thing to note is that vertices that are not in the breadth-first tree (as is the case of 0) are unreachable from the root vertex.

We previously saw how to perform the breadth-first search on trees. BFS on graphs is similar, but we need to keep track of explored nodes so that we don't get stuck in cycles. In order to implement breadth-first search, we will assume that our graph is represented using adjacency lists.

We will attach certain attributes to each vertex in the graph that will allow us to guide our search and later construct the breadth-first tree. We will also use a first-in, first-out queue (covered in Chapter 2, *Sorting Algorithms and Fundamental Data Structures*) to manage the set of discovered vertices. The following code snippet illustrates the implementation of breadth-first search:

```
Queue<Integer> q = new LinkedList<>();
q.add(start);
while (!q.isEmpty()) {
  int current = q.remove();
  for (int i = 0; i < this.adj[current].size(); i++) {
    int next = this.adj[current].get(i);
    if (!visited[next]) {
      visited[next] = true;
      parent[next] = current;
      q.add(next);
    }
  }
}
```

Snippet 6.4: Implementation of breadth-first search. Source class name: BFS.Graph

Go to `https://goo.gl/VqrQWM` to access this code.

Let's focus on the implementation of the BFS function. We will start by initializing a couple of auxiliary arrays: `parent` and `visited`. The first one will hold, at `parent[i]`, the parent of node `i` in the breadth-first tree. The second one will tell us, at `visited[i]`, whether or not vertex `i` has been discovered. We start by discovering the starting node and adding it to a queue. The queue will keep those vertices that have been discovered but not yet expanded. As such, while there are still elements in the queue, we will take its first element, go through its adjacent vertices, and discover those that haven't already been discovered, adding them to the queue.

When the queue becomes empty, we're sure of having expanded all vertices that are reachable from the starting vertex.

In the previous implementation, we've returned the array of parent nodes of the breadth-first tree in the `bfs()` function, allowing us to reconstruct the paths. If not necessary, you could just return the size of paths, or any other information we might be interested in extracting from the breadth-first search traversal.

In the `bfs()` method, we're sure of enqueuing, and hence dequeuing, each vertex at most once. As such, the total time dedicated to queue operations is $O(V)$. After dequeuing each vertex, we scan its adjacency list. Since we dequeue each vertex at most once, we scan each adjacency list at most once. As the sum of lengths of all the adjacency lists is $O(E)$, the total time spent in scanning adjacency lists is $O(E)$. Therefore, the BFS procedure has an initialization time of $O(V)$ and a total running time of $O(V + E)$, running in linear time to the size of the adjacency list representation of G.

As we will see in later sections, the BFS procedure is the archetype for many important graph algorithms.

Depth-First Search

Given a graph $G = (V, E)$ and a source vertex s, depth-first search explores the edges of the graph by going "deeper" in the graph whenever possible. **Depth-First Search (DFS)** explores edges adjacent to the most recently discovered vertex v that still has unexplored edges whose head is adjacent to it. Once all of v's edges have been explored, the search "backtracks" to explore edges, leaving the vertex from which v was discovered. The process continues until all vertices that are reachable from the original source vertex have been discovered.

If any undiscovered vertices remain, then DFS selects one of them as a new source, and it repeats the search from that source. While it may seem odd that BFS limits itself to vertices reachable from a single source whereas DFS considers multiple sources, the reason behind it is related to the applications of these searches.

BFS is usually used to find shortest-path distances while DFS is often used as a subroutine in another algorithm, which we shall see when we explore the cycle detection problem.

Similar to BFS, when we discover a vertex v during the scan of the adjacency list of an already discovered vertex, we record its parent attribute. Since we mentioned that we explore different sources, the parent subgraph produced by DFS is, unlike the breadth-first tree, a forest (that is, a set of trees).

In order to illustrate this, let's look at a run of DFS for the directed graph of *Figure 6.1*, starting at *node 2*, in the following table:

Step	Current Node	Discovered	Expanded	Undiscovered	Forest
0	2	{2}	{}	{0, 1, 3, 4, 5}	
1	4	{2, 4}	{}	{0, 1, 3, 5}	
2	3	{2, 4, 3}	{}	{0, 1, 5}	
3	1	{2, 4, 3, 1}	{}	{0, 5}	
4	3	{2, 4, 3, 1}	{1}	{0, 5}	
5	4	{2, 4, 3, 1}	{1, 4}	{0, 5}	
6	2	{2, 4, 3, 1}	{1, 4, 3}	{0, 5}	

Step	Current Node	Discovered	Expanded	Undiscovered	Forest
6	5	{2, 4, 3, 1, 5}	{1, 4, 3}	{0}	
7	2	{2, 4, 3, 1, 5}	{1, 4, 3, 5}	{0}	
8	0	{2, 4, 3, 1, 5, 0}	{1, 4, 3, 5, 2}	{}	
9	-	{2, 4, 3, 1, 5, 0}	{1, 4, 3, 5, 2, 0}	{}	

Table 6.4: A run of DFS on the directed graph of Figure 6.1, starting at node 2

Note that the results of DFS may depend on the order in which the vertices are examined. In the previous case, we started with 2 and always went for the lowest-numbered vertex in the adjacency list of a vertex first. If we had started with vertex 0, we would have a different forest. In practice, we can usually use any DFS result with equivalent results.

We previously saw how to perform DFS on trees. DFS on graphs is similar, but we need to keep track of explored nodes so that we don't get stuck in cycles.

In order to implement DFS, we will assume that our graph is represented using adjacency lists. We will attach certain attributes to each vertex in the graph, which will allow us to guide our search and later construct the depth-first forest. The following code snippet illustrates the implementation of depth-first search:

```
public void dfsVisit(int u, boolean[] visited, int[] parent) {
    visited[u] = true;
    for (int i = 0; i < adj[u].size(); i++) {
        int next = adj[u].get(i);
        if (!visited[next]) {
            parent[next] = u;
            dfsVisit(next, visited, parent);
        }
    }
}
```

Snippet 6.5: Implementation of depth-first search. Source class name:dfs.Graph.

 Go to `https://goo.gl/saZYQp` to access this code.

The DFS procedure works by initializing all vertices as not visited, and setting their parents to *-1* (meaning that they have no parent). Then, we find the first undiscovered vertex and visit it. In each visit, we start by recording the vertex as visited and then going through its adjacency list. There, we are looking for vertices not yet discovered. Once we find one, we visit it. Looking at the previous implementation, we see that the loops inside DFS take time $O(V)$, as they run for each vertex in the graph. We can also see that the dfsVisit() method is called exactly once for each vertex. During the execution of dfsVisit(), the loop scanning the adjacency list executes in time proportional to the size of the vertex's adjacency list. Since we said before that dfsVisit() is called exactly once for each vertex, the total time spent in the loop is proportional to the sum of the sizes of all adjacency lists, that is, $O(E)$. Therefore, the total running time of DFS is $O(V + E)$.

In the DFS method, we're returning the parent array, but the return type of this routine is usually adapted depending on the larger task that a more general algorithm that uses DFS is trying to achieve. We'll see DFS adapted to our specific needs in the next section.

Cycle Detection

A useful application of DFS is determining whether or not a graph is acyclic (that is, it does not contain cycles). In order to do so, it's important to define four types of edges in terms of the depth-first forest produced by DFS. They are as follows:

- **Tree edges**: They are edges in the depth-first forest. An edge can only be a tree edge if it was the one explored when first discovering a vertex.
- **Back edges**: They are edges connecting a vertex to an ancestor in a depth-first tree. Self-loops (which may occur in directed graphs) are back edges.
- **Forward edges**: They are edges that do not belong to a depth-first tree but connect a vertex to one of its descendants in a depth-first tree. Forward edges are therefore edges that weren't used when performing the DFS, but connect vertices u and v in a depth-first tree provided that v is a descendant of u in the tree.
- **Cross edges**: They are all other edges. They can go between vertices in the same depth-first tree or they can go between vertices in different depth-first trees. They are therefore edges that weren't used when performing the depth-first search, but connect vertices that don't share an ancestor relationship in the same tree or vertices in different trees.

Having classified edges, it is possible to show that a directed graph is acyclic if and only if a DFS does not produce back edges. If a depth-first search produces a back edge (u, v), then vertex v is an ancestor of vertex u in the depth-first forest. Therefore, G contains a path from v to u, and (u, v) completes a cycle. This algorithm is generalizable for undirected graphs. In undirected graphs, if we find a back edge (u, v) and v is not the parent of u in the depth-first forest, then we are in the presence of a cycle.

Activity: Using BFS to Find the Shortest Path Out of a Maze

Scenario

Our maze is an H by W rectangle, represented by an array of size H of W-sized strings. Each character in a string can either be '#' or '.'. '#' represents a wall, which we cannot cross, and '.' represents a free space, which we can cross. The border of the maze is always filled with '#' except for one square, which represents the exit. For example, the following is a valid maze:

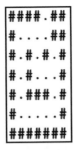

```
####.##
#....##
#.#.#.#
#.#...#
#.###.#
#.....#
#######
```

Find the total number of steps to exit the maze, when supplied with a starting point *(i, j)* (with *(0, 0)* being the upper-left point and *(H, W)* being the lower-right point).

Aim

To use BFS to find the shortest path out of a given maze.

Prerequisites

- Implement the `distToExit()` method of the `Maze` class in the source code, which returns the integer distance from that point to the exit of the maze. It is available at the following URL:
  `https://github.com/TrainingByPackt/Data-Structures-and-Algorithms-in-Java/blob/master/src/main/java/com/packt/datastructuresandalg/lesson6/activity/maze/Maze.java`
- Assume that the points supplied to `distToExit()` are valid (that is, they're not inside walls)
- Remember that we can only move in the cardinal directions (North, South, East, and West)

Steps for Completion

1. Encode the maze representation to a graph representation
2. Apply the BFS implementation shown in the preceding section (with a small modification to account for distances), or you can build the graph as you go
3. Since you know that there are at most four outward edges for a given vertex, compute their positions as you go

In this section, we've introduced two different ways to traverse a graph—**breadth-first search (BFS)** and **depth-first search (DFS)**. We've seen how to use BFS to find the single-source shortest path in unweighted graphs and how to use DFS to find cycles in a graph. In the next section, we will be looking at two different algorithms to find shortest paths in a graph.

Calculating Shortest Paths

The shortest path is a path between two vertices so that the sum of the weights of the edges that constitute the path is minimized. The shortest path problem has many applications in the real world, from finding directions on mapping applications to minimizing the moves to solve a puzzle.

In this section, we shall look at two different strategies for computing shortest paths: one that finds the shortest paths from a single source to every other vertex in the graph, and another that finds shortest paths between all pairs of vertices in a graph.

Single Source Shortest Path: Dijkstra's Algorithm

When we explored BFS, we saw that it was able to solve the shortest path problem for unweighted graphs, or graphs whose edges have the same (positive) weight. What if we are dealing with weighted graphs? Can we do better? We shall see that Dijkstra's algorithm provides an improvement over the ideas presented in BFS and that it is an efficient algorithm for solving the single-source shortest path problem. One restriction for working with Dijkstra's algorithm is that edges' weights have to be positive. This is usually not a big issue since most graphs represent entities modeled by edges with positive weights. Nonetheless, there are algorithms capable of solving the problem for negative weights. Since the use case for negative edges is less common, those algorithms are outside the scope of this book.

Dijkstra's algorithm, conceived by Edsger W. Dijkstra in 1956, maintains a set S of vertices whose final shortest-path weights from the source s have already been determined. The algorithm repeatedly selects the vertex u with the minimum shortest-path estimate, adds it to set S, and uses the outward edges from that vertex to update the estimates from vertices not yet in set S. In order to see this in action, let's consider the directed graph of *Figure 6.5*:

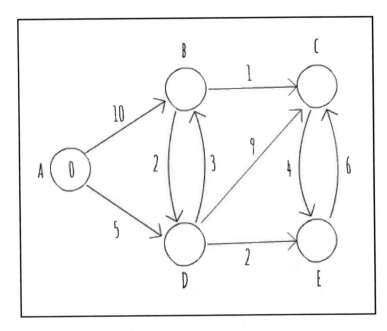

Figure 6.5: A sample weighted directed graph

The graph is composed of five vertices (*A, B, C, D,* and *E*) and 10 edges. We're interested in finding the shortest paths, starting at vertex *A*. Note that A is already marked as *0*, meaning that the current distance from *A* to *A* is zero. The other vertices don't have distances associated with them yet. It is common to use an estimate of infinity as the starting estimate for the distance of nodes not yet seen. The following table shows a run of Dijkstra's algorithm for the graph of *Figure 6.5*, identifying the current vertex being selected and how it updates the estimates for vertices not yet seen:

Step	Explanation
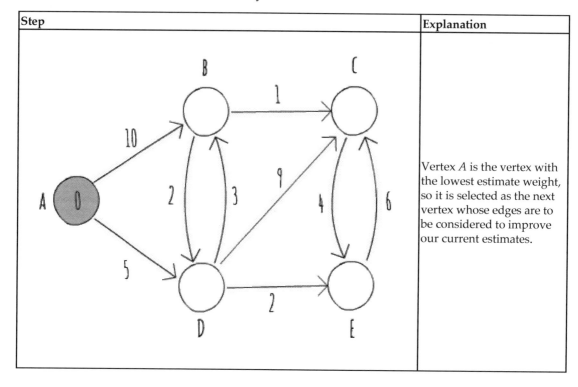	Vertex *A* is the vertex with the lowest estimate weight, so it is selected as the next vertex whose edges are to be considered to improve our current estimates.

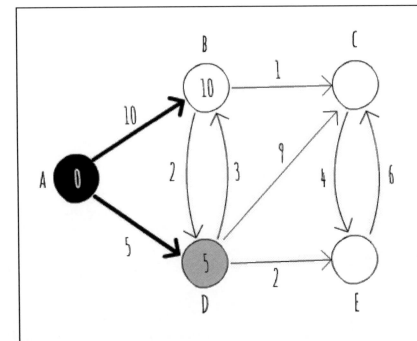

We use the outward edges from vertex *A* to update our estimates for vertices *B* and *D*. Afterwards, we add *A* to set *S*, avoiding a repeated visit to it. From the edges not yet visited, the one with the lowest estimate is now *D*, which shall be selected to visit next. Note that we also mark those edges that belong to our estimate shortest path in bold.

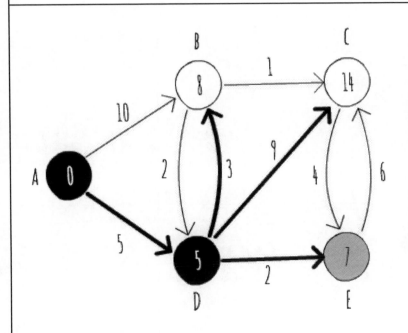

By exploring the outward edges from vertex *D*, we were able to improve our estimate for vertex *B*, so we update it accordingly and now consider a different edge for the shortest path. We were also able to discover vertices *C* and *E*, which become potential candidates to visit next. Since *E* is the one with the shorter estimate weight, we visit it next.

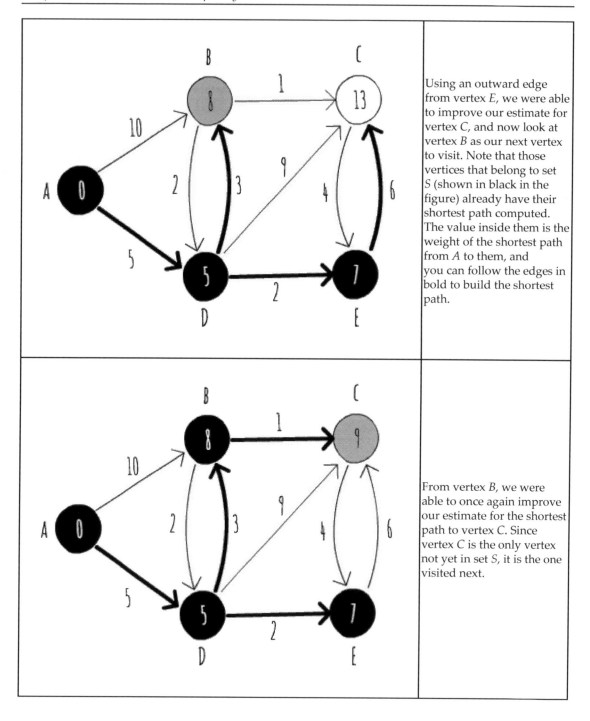

Using an outward edge from vertex E, we were able to improve our estimate for vertex C, and now look at vertex B as our next vertex to visit. Note that those vertices that belong to set S (shown in black in the figure) already have their shortest path computed. The value inside them is the weight of the shortest path from A to them, and you can follow the edges in bold to build the shortest path.

From vertex B, we were able to once again improve our estimate for the shortest path to vertex C. Since vertex C is the only vertex not yet in set S, it is the one visited next.

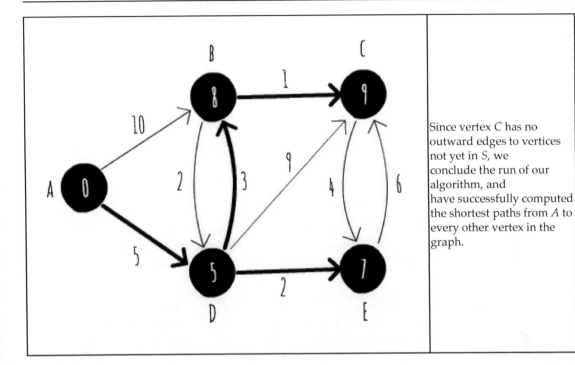

Since vertex *C* has no outward edges to vertices not yet in *S*, we conclude the run of our algorithm, and have successfully computed the shortest paths from *A* to every other vertex in the graph.

Table 6.5: A run of Dijkstra's algorithm for the weighted directed graph of Figure 6.5

Now that we've seen a run of Dijkstra's algorithm, let's try to put it in code and analyze its runtime performance. We will use an adjacency list representation for our graph, as it helps us when trying to explore the outward edges of a given vertex. The following code snippet shows a possible implementation of Dijkstra's algorithm as previously described:

```
while (!notVisited.isEmpty()) {
  Vertex v = getBestEstimate(notVisited);
  notVisited.remove(v);
  visited.add(v);
  for (Edge e : adj[v.u]) {
    if (!visited.contains(e.v)) {
      Vertex next = vertices[e.v];
      if (v.distance + e.weight < next.distance) {
        next.distance = v.distance + e.weight;
        parent[next.u] = v.u;
      }
    }
  }
}
```

Snippet 6.6: Implementation of Dijkstra's algorithm. Source class name: Dijkstra

Go to `https://goo.gl/P7p5Ce` to access this code.

The Dijkstra method starts by initializing two sets:

- One for visited vertices
- One for unvisited vertices

The set of visited vertices corresponds to the set we previously named as *S*, and we use the one of not visited vertices to keep track of vertices to explore.

We then initialize each vertex with an estimated distance equal to `Integer.MAX_VALUE`, representing a value of "infinity" for our use case. We also use a parent array to keep track of parent vertices in the shortest path, so that we can later recreate the path from the source to each vertex.

The main loop runs for each vertex, while we still have vertices not yet visited. For each run, it selects the "best" vertex to explore. In this case, the "best" vertex is the one with the smallest distance of the vertices not visited so far (the `getBestEstimate()` function simply scans all vertices in the `notVisited()` set for the one satisfying the requirement).

Then, it adds the vertex to the set of visited vertices and updates the estimate distances for not visited vertices. When we run out of vertices to visit, we build our paths by recursively visiting the parent array.

Analyzing the runtime of the previous implementation, we can see that we have an initialization step that's proportional to the number of vertices in the graph, hence running in *O(V)*.

The main loop of the algorithm runs once for each vertex, so it is bounded by at least *O(V)*. Inside the main loop, we determine the next vertex to visit and then scan its adjacency list to update the estimate distances. Updating the distances takes time proportional to *O(1)*, and since we scan each vertex's adjacency list only once, we take time proportional to *O(E)*, updating estimate distances. We're left with the time spent selecting the next vertex to visit. Unfortunately, the `getBestEstimate()` method needs to scan through all the unvisited vertices, and is therefore bounded by *O(V)*. The total running time of our implementation of Dijkstra's algorithm is therefore *O(V²+E)*.

Even though some parts of our implementation seem difficult to optimize, it looks like we can do better when selecting the next vertex to visit. If we could have access to a data structure that was capable of storing our vertices sorted by lower estimated distance and provided efficient insert and remove operations, then we could reduce the *O(V)* time spent inside the getBestEstimate method.

In Chapter 4, *Algorithm Design Paradigms*, we briefly discussed a data structure used in Huffman coding named the priority queue, which is just what we need for this job. The following code snippet implements a more efficient version of Dijkstra's algorithm, using a priority queue:

```
PriorityQueue<Node> pq = new PriorityQueue<>();
pq.add(new Node(source, 0));
while (!pq.isEmpty()) {
  Node v = pq.remove();
  if (!vertices[v.u].visited) {
    vertices[v.u].visited = true;
    for (Edge e : adj[v.u]) {
      Vertex next = vertices[e.v];
      if (v.distance + e.weight < next.distance) {
        next.distance = v.distance + e.weight;
        parent[next.u] = v.u;
        pq.add(new Node(next.u, next.distance));
      }
    }
  }
}
```

Snippet 6.7: Implementation of Dijkstra's algorithm using a priority queue. Source class name: DijkstraWithPQ

 Go to https://goo.gl/3rtZCQ to access this code.

In this second implementation, we no longer keep sets for visited and not visited vertices. Instead, we rely on a priority queue that will be storing our distance estimates while we run the algorithm.

When we are exploring the outward edges from a given vertex, we therefore add a new entry to the priority queue in case we are able to improve our distance estimate.

Adding and removing an element from our priority queue takes $O(logN)$ time, N being the number of elements in the queue. Do note that we can have the same vertex inserted more than once in the priority queue. That's why we check if we've visited it before expanding its edges.

Since we will visit the instance for that vertex with shorter estimate distance, it's safe to ignore the ones that come after it. However, that means that operations on our priority queue are not bounded by $O(logV)$, but $O(log E)$ instead (assuming that there's a connected graph).

Therefore, the total runtime of this implementation is $O((V + E)logE)$. It's still possible to improve this running time by using a priority queue implementation with better asymptotic bounds (such as a Fibonacci heap), but its implementation is out of the scope of this book.

One last thing to note about Dijkstra's algorithm is how it borrows ideas from BFS (the algorithm structure is very similar to Dijkstra's, but we end up using a priority queue instead of a normal queue) and that it is a very good example of a greedy algorithm: Dijkstra's algorithm makes the locally optimum choice (for example, it chooses the vertex with the minimum estimated distance) in order to arrive at a global optimum.

All Pairs Shortest Paths: Floyd-Warshall Algorithm

Sometimes, it might be necessary to compute the shortest paths between all pairs of vertices. For example, we might be interested in building a table of distances. One way to do that is to perform a single source shortest path for every vertex of the graph. If you use Dijkstra's algorithm for that, we end up with a runtime of $O(V*(V + E)logE)$.

In this subsection, we shall explore an algorithm capable of solving the all pairs shortest paths problem in $O(V^3)$ time, with a remarkably simple and elegant implementation.

The algorithm we are about to study, more commonly referred to as the Floyd-Warshall algorithm, was published in its current form by Robert Floyd in 1962. However, in its essence, it follows the same ideas published by Bernard Roy in 1959 and Stephen Warshall in 1962.

The algorithm uses the adjacency matrix representation and follows a dynamic programming approach. The basic idea behind it is that, when we're trying to compute the shortest-path distance between vertex i and vertex j, we try to use an intermediate vertex, k. We want to use an intermediate vertex so that doing the path from i to k and then from k to j shortens the currently computed shortest path between i and j. If we find such a vertex, then the best path we're able to compute so far between i and j must go through k. All that we need to do is, for each k, see if using it improves the shortest path between i and j, for all possible i and j.

In order to see that in practice, let's use the directed graph of *Figure 6.5* that we used to illustrate Dijkstra's algorithm. The graph of *Figure 6.5* has the adjacency matrix representation of the following table:

	A	B	C	D	E
A	0	10	∞	5	∞
B	∞	0	1	2	∞
C	∞	∞	0	∞	4
D	∞	3	9	0	2
E	∞	∞	6	∞	0

Table 6.6: Adjacency matrix representation of the directed graph of Figure 6.5

The adjacency matrix representation serves as the starting point for the Floyd-Warshall algorithm, and we iterate through it until we're left with a matrix of the weights of the shortest paths between each pair of vertices. In order to do so, let's start with vertex A, considering it as an intermediate vertex for shortest paths. Unfortunately, vertex A doesn't have inward edges, meaning that it can't be used as an intermediate vertex for shortest paths. Using vertex B, we can improve the distance from A to C ($10 + 1 < \infty$), and we can use it to go from A to D, but not improve the overall distance. We can also use it to improve the distance from D to C ($3 + 1 < 9$). Therefore, after considering B as an intermediate vertex, we're left with the distance matrix of the following table:

	A	B	C	D	E
A	0	10	11	5	∞
B	∞	0	1	2	∞
C	∞	∞	0	∞	4
D	∞	3	4	0	2
E	∞	∞	6	∞	0

Table 6.7: Distance matrix after considering B as an intermediate vertex

Now, we are going to look at vertex C. Using vertex C, we can improve the distance from A to E $(11 + 4 < \infty)$ and B to E $(1 + 4 < \infty)$:

	A	B	C	D	E
A	0	10	11	5	15
B	∞	0	1	2	5
C	∞	∞	0	∞	4
D	∞	3	4	0	2
E	∞	∞	6	∞	0

Table 6.8: Distance matrix after considering C as an intermediate vertex

Using vertex D, we can improve the distance from A to B $(5 + 3 < 10)$, A to C $(5 + 4 < 11)$, A to E $(5 + 2 < 15)$, and B to E $(2 + 2 < 5)$:

	A	B	C	D	E
A	0	8	9	5	7
B	∞	0	1	2	4
C	∞	∞	0	∞	4
D	∞	3	4	0	2
E	∞	∞	6	∞	0

Table 6.9: Distance matrix after considering D as an intermediate vertex

Using vertex E, we cannot improve any distance, so *Table 6.9* already has the weights for the shortest paths between all pairs of vertices. Implementing the Floyd-Warshall algorithm is very simple, as the following code snippet demonstrates:

```
public void run() {
    for (int k = 0; k < adj.length; k++) {
        for (int i = 0; i < adj.length; i++) {
            if (adj[i][k] >= Integer.MAX_VALUE)
                continue;
            for (int j = 0; j < adj.length; j++) {
                if (adj[k][j] >= Integer.MAX_VALUE)
                    continue;
                adj[i][j] = Math.min(adj[i][j], adj[i][k] + adj[k][j]);
            }
        }
    }
}
```

Snippet 6.8: Implementation of Floyd Warshall's algorithm. Source class name: FloydWarshall

Go to `https://goo.gl/SQxdL2` to access this code.

Looking at the implementation, the runtime of $O(V^3)$ becomes obvious. One alternative to the Floyd-Warshall algorithm is running Dijkstra's algorithm for each vertex in the graph (so that we end up with all pairwise shortest paths). Given that its complexity is closer to multiple applications of Dijkstra's algorithm for dense graphs, the Floyd-Warshall algorithm is frequently used in practice.

Activity: Improving Floyd-Warshall's Algorithm to Reconstruct the Shortest Path

Scenario

Improve Floyd-Warshall's algorithm so that we're able to reconstruct the shortest path between two given nodes after running the algorithm, using the predecessor matrix.

Aim

To construct a shortest path between the two vertices using the predecessor matrix.

Prerequisite

 The predecessor matrix is used to compute the shortest path between two given vertices. Each cell of the predecessor matrix P_{ij} should be either empty (meaning that there is no path between i and j), or equal to some index k (meaning that vertex k is the one that precedes j in the shortest path between i and j). As such, we need to update our predecessor matrix whenever we use an intermediate vertex.

Implement the `run()` method of the Floyd-Warshall class that shall compute the shortest paths for the current graph and populate the path matrix, used later in the `path()` method to return the path between two given vertices. The method is available at the following URL:

```
https://github.com/TrainingByPackt/Data-Structures-and-Algorithms-in-Java/blob/
master/src/main/java/com/packt/datastructuresandalg/lesson6/activity/
floydwarshall/FloydWarshall.java
```

Steps for Completion

1. Adapt the implementation shown in *Snippet 6.8* of the Floyd-Warshall algorithm to update the path matrix
2. Use it to reconstruct the paths similarly to what we have previously shown in the implementation of Dijkstra's algorithm

In this section, we've introduced the shortest paths problem and visited two different algorithms to solve it: one for single source shortest paths (Dijkstra's algorithm), and another for all pairs shortest paths (Floyd-Warshall). We've shown how different implementations of Dijkstra's algorithm can affect its running time. For both algorithms, we've also shown how to reconstruct shortest paths using a parent array and a predecessor matrix, respectively.

Prime Numbers in Algorithms

A prime number is a natural number greater than one whose only divisors are one and the number itself.

Prime numbers play a very important role in the fundamental theorem of arithmetic: every natural number greater than one is either a prime or a product of primes. Nowadays, number-theoretic algorithms are widely used, mainly due to cryptographic schemes based on large prime numbers. Most of those cryptographic schemes are based on the fact that we can efficiently find large primes, but we cannot factor the product of those large primes efficiently. As seen before, prime numbers play an important role in the implementation of hash tables.

Sieve of Eratosthenes

The sieve of Eratosthenes is a simple and ancient algorithm to find all prime numbers up to a given limit. If we want to find all prime numbers up to N, we start by creating a list of consecutive integers from 2 to N (2, 3, 4, 5... N), initially unmarked. Let's use p to denote the smallest unmarked number. Then, we select the smallest unmarked number p that is larger than the last p. In the first iteration, p will be two. Afterwards, by increments of p, we mark elements in the list from $2p$ until Mp so that $Mp <= N$.

We repeat this strategy until it is impossible to mark more numbers in the list. At the end of the run, all the unmarked numbers are prime numbers. It is easy to see that all unmarked numbers will be the ones for which we couldn't find a divisor other than the number itself and 1, and are therefore prime numbers.

Prime Factorization

Prime factorization is determining the prime factors of a given number. It is very difficult to build a general-purpose algorithm for this computationally hard problem. A general purpose algorithm that is commonly used to factorize primes was introduced in Chapter 1, *Algorithms and Complexities*. Its basic idea is to iterate through possible factors attempting to divide the number.

Start with 2; while the number is divisible by 2, keep dividing it, and add 2 to the list of factors. Afterwards, the number must be odd, so start a loop that checks for possible factors from 3 to the square root of the number.

Since we've already covered even numbers, you can do increments of 2 in this loop (there's no need to check 4, 6, 8, and so on once you've already checked 2). Once you find a suitable divisor, add the number to the list of factors and divide it until it is possible. At the end of this step, if we are left with a number greater than 2, then it is a prime number and therefore a prime factor of itself.

Activity: Implementing the Sieve of Eratosthenes

Scenario

Implementing the sieve of Eratosthenes algorithm to find all prime numbers up to a given limit.

Aim

To develop a code in Java for implementing the sieve of Eratosthenes.

Prerequisites

- Implement the isPrime() method of the SieveOfEratosthenes class that should return true if the number is prime, and false otherwise. It is available at the following URL:
  https://github.com/TrainingByPackt/Data-Structures-and-Algorithms-in-Java/blob/master/src/main/java/com/packt/datastructuresandalg/lesson7/activity/sieve/SieveOfEratosthenes.java
- Consider building the sieve in the class constructor

Other Concepts in Graphs

In this chapter, we covered ways of representing and traversing a graph and looked at shortest path algorithms. Graphs are also an optimal data structure for some problems we haven't mentioned yet. This section aims to introduce some of them.

Minimum Spanning Trees

A minimum spanning tree of a graph is a subset of the set of edges E of a connected graph that connects all vertices together, without any cycles and with the minimum total edge weight. It is a tree because every two vertices in it are connected by exactly one path.

In order to understand the applicability of minimum spanning trees, consider the problem of a telecommunications company that is moving into a new neighborhood. The company wants to connect all the houses, but also wants to minimize the length of cable that it uses in order to cut costs. One way to solve the problem is by computing the minimum spanning tree of a graph whose vertices are the houses of the neighborhood, and the edges between houses are weighted according to the distance between them.

There are many algorithms to solve the minimum spanning tree problem. Two of the most famous are Prim's and Kruskal's.

Prim's algorithm is a greedy algorithm that repeatedly selects the edge of smaller weights that connect some edge not yet in the spanning tree with some edge already in the spanning tree. Its runtime depends on the implementation, but it's possible to achieve a runtime of $O(VlogE)$. It can be implemented similarly to Dijkstra's algorithm. We start with one vertex chosen arbitrarily to be part of the tree. All edges that connect to this "starting" vertex are added to a set of candidate edges that are sorted according to the edges' weights. While we still have vertices to add to the tree, we repeatedly select the edge with the smaller weight from the list of candidate edges that connects to a vertex not yet in the tree, and repeat the process for the new vertex.

Kruskal's algorithm is also a greedy algorithm that uses a disjoint-set data structure. A disjoint-set data structure, or union-find data structure, is a data structure that tracks elements that are partitioned into a number of non-overlapping subsets. It provides an efficient way to merge two sets and check whether two elements belong to the same set.

The idea of Kruskal's algorithm is to reduce a forest (for example, a set of trees) to a single tree, using a disjoint-set data structure to keep track of trees. We start with one tree for each vertex, including only one vertex. While we have more than one tree, we select the edge of the smallest weight that connects two different trees (we don't want to produce a cycle), and join the two trees together. At the end, the resultant tree will be the one whose total edge weight is minimized. The running time of Kruskal's algorithm is also *O(VlogE)*.

A* Search

The *A** search algorithm is a very common algorithm when solving path-finding problems. It also solves the shortest path problem, enhancing Dijkstra's algorithm with the introduction of a heuristic to guide the search. A heuristic is a practical estimate of a given cost, not guaranteed to be optimal or perfect, but sufficient for the immediate goals, or to guide a search. Its basic idea is that, when adding this heuristic to the estimated distance already computed for a node, one can guide the search towards the goal and avoid visiting certain vertices.

For example, if we use the Euclidean distance (for example, the straight line distance between two points) from our location to the exit of a given maze, we can guide the search towards that and avoid visiting certain unnecessary positions.

Maximum Flow

Some directed weighted graphs can be seen as flow networks. In a flow network, edge weights represent capacities and each edge receives a flow that can't exceed the edge's capacity. The labels on the edges represent the used and total capacity of the edge. The maximum flow attempts to find a feasible flow through the network that is maximum, considering a single source (where the initial flow starts) and single sink (where the flow ends). The maximum flow problem allows one to solve related problems like pair wise assignment. There are various algorithms to solve the maximum flow problem. Three of the most famous ones are the FordFulkerson algorithm, the Edmonds-Karp algorithm, and Dinic's algorithm.

The idea behind the Ford-Fulkerson algorithm is to repeatedly find augmenting paths in the flow network. An augmenting path is a path that still has an available capacity. While it is possible to find augmenting paths, one can add a flow through the path equal to its capacity and repeat the process. Ford-Fulkerson algorithm runs in $O(Ef)$, f being the maximum flow of the graph. The Edmonds-Karp algorithm improves on the Ford-Fulkerson algorithm by always selecting the augmenting path that is shortest. The runtime complexity of the Edmonds-Karp algorithm is $O(VE^2)$, independent of the maximum flow value. Dinic's algorithm runs in $O(V^2E)$ time, also building on shortest augmenting paths, but uses some concepts that make it more suitable for sparse graphs.

Understanding Complexity Classes of Problems

Nearly all of the algorithms introduced so far run in polynomial time (for instance, on inputs of size n, their worst-case running time is $O(n^k)$ for constant k). However, there are problems that simply cannot be solved or for which a polynomial-time algorithm hasn't been found yet.

An example of a problem that cannot be solved is the halting problem. The halting problem is the problem of determining, from the description of a computer program and an input, whether the program will finish running or continue to run forever. Alan Turing proved that a general algorithm to solve the halting problem for all pairs of (program, input) cannot exist.

It is common to call problems solvable by polynomial-time algorithms (for instance, those whose worst-case running time is $O(n^k)$ for constant k) as "tractable", or "easy", and problems that require a super-polynomial-time algorithm (for instance, those whose running time is not bounded above by any polynomial) as "intractable", or "hard".

There is a class of problems, called **NP-Complete (NPC)** problems, and no one has yet found a polynomial-time algorithm to solve them. However, no one has yet been able to prove that no polynomial-time algorithm can exist for any of them.

There is another class of problems, called **NP** problems, whose solutions are verifiable in polynomial time. This means that, given a problem, and a possible solution to it, one can verify if the solution is correct in polynomial time.

All problems in P are also in NP. NPC consists of problems that belong to the NP class and to the NP-hard class. A problem is NP-hard if an algorithm for solving it can be translated into one for solving a NP problem.

One of the deepest open research problems in theoretical computer science is whether *P* is really different from NP (for instance, *P != NP*).

Examples of NPC problems are as follows:

- Finding the longest path in the graph
- Finding a path in a graph that visits all vertices exactly once (known as a Hamiltonian path)

A common example of an NP-hard problem is finding the shortest path in a graph that visits all vertices exactly once and returns to the starting point. The problem consists of finding the Hamiltonian cycle of the smallest weight, and is often described as the traveling salesman problem as it models the problem of a salesman that needs to visit all cities and return to his hometown.

Summary

In this chapter, we have introduced graphs, formalized what they are and shown two different ways to represent them in computer programs. Afterwards, we took a look at ways of traversing graphs, using them as building blocks for building more complex algorithms on top. Then, we looked at two different algorithms for finding shortest paths in a graph.

At the end of this book, we provide pointers for curious students to study on their own. The world of data structures and algorithms is vast and requires a type of mathematical reasoning for which some study and practice is required. However, one of the most rewarding feelings in the life of a software engineer is coming up with a clever algorithms to solve a complex problems.

Other Books You May Enjoy

If you enjoyed this book, you may be interested in these other products by Packt:

Everyday Data Structures
William Smith

ISBN: 978-1-78712-104-1

- A rapid overview of data types, applications for each type, best practices and high-level variations between platforms
- Review the most common data structures and build working examples in the languages used for mobile platform software development
- Understand advanced data structure concepts such as generic collections, searching and sorting algorithms, and recursion
- Learn to use Stacks (LIFO) and queues (FIFO) in your daily application
- Add/remove objects and nest arrays and dictionaries within another dictionary and understand why such architecture is often preferred or necessary
- Get acquainted with the tree structures such as heap, binary, and graphs, apply them to work
- Unleash the power of different sorting techniques such as bubble sort, quick sort, merge sort, insertion sort, and radix sort
- Perform searching operations on arrays, heaps, graphs, and binary trees in different languages

Java 9 Data Structures and Algorithms
Debasish Ray Chawdhuri

ISBN: 978-1-78588-934-9

- Understand the fundamentals of algorithms, data structures, and measurement of complexity
- Find out what general purpose data structures are, including arrays, linked lists, double ended linked lists, and circular lists
- Get a grasp on the basics of abstract data types—stack, queue, and double ended queue
- See how to use recursive functions and immutability while understanding and in terms of recursion
- Handle reactive programming and its related data structures
- Use binary search, sorting, and efficient sorting—quicksort and merge sort
- Work with the important concept of trees and list all nodes of the tree, traversal of tree, search trees, and balanced search trees
- Apply advanced general purpose data structures, priority queue-based sorting, and random access immutable linked lists
- Gain a better understanding of the concept of graphs, directed and undirected graphs, undirected trees, and much more

Leave a Review - Let Other Readers Know What You Think

Please share your thoughts on this book with others by leaving a review on the site that you bought it from. If you purchased the book from Amazon, please leave us an honest review on this book's Amazon page. This is vital so that other potential readers can see and use your unbiased opinion to make purchasing decisions, we can understand what our customers think about our products, and our authors can see your feedback on the title that they have worked with Packt to create. It will only take a few minutes of your time, but is valuable to other potential customers, our authors, and Packt. Thank you!

Index

Made in the USA
Columbia, SC
15 January 2021